This is an important book wit........ .... human nature, and the vast lattice of nature that embraces all beings."

—Joan Halifax
author, *The Fruitful Darkness:*
Reconnecting with the Body of the Earth

❧

Inner Passages Outer Journeys adds another level of healing wisdom to the merging paradigm of health. [The author] reminds us that the environment is our extended body and that when given the opportunity, Nature is the ultimate healer, returning us to wholeness."

—David Simon, M.D.
Medical Director of the Chopra Center for Well Being

❧

We have preserved wilderness areas, like books in a library—but 'reading' them will require more spiritual sensitivity. This book will help."

—Roderick Frazier Nash
Professor Emeritus and author,
Wilderness and the American Mind

ABOUT THE AUTHOR

Dave Cumes, M.D., was born in South Africa and has been a wilderness traveler most of his life. A specialist in urologic surgery, he has taught at Stanford Medical Center and currently has a private practice in Santa Barbara, California.

In contrast to his classical training in a profession that relies so heavily on science and analytical reasoning, he has pursued a personal quest that evokes intuitive and introspective capabilities. After spending time with the San hunter-gatherers of the Kalahari desert, he realized how profound a role wilderness can play in personal restoration and transformation. Since his original contact with the San, he has traveled extensively, studied a variety of philosophies and developed his own approach to tapping the healing power of nature and facilitating the experience of "wilderness rapture."

Cumes shares his insight through a company he founded called Inward Bound. He leads groups on healing journeys to Peru, South Aftrica, and the Sinai Desert. As a graduate of the National Outdoor Leadership School, he has formal training as a wilderness guide, which is essential for the "outward bound" aspects of the "inward bound" journeys he leads. In response to growing interest in these inner journeys, he has presented his experiences through lectures and slide presentations. Over the years, he has addressed people from diverse backgrounds and interests, including psychologists, nurses, and physicians, as well as wilderness enthusiasts and the general public.

TO WRITE TO THE AUTHOR

If you would like to contact the author or would like more information about this book, please write to him in care of Llewellyn Worldwide. We cannot guarantee every letter will be answered, but all will be forwarded. Please write to:

Dave Cumes, M.D.
C/o Llewellyn Worldwide
P.O. Box 64383, Dept. K195-3
St. Paul, MN 55164-0383 U.S.A.

For more information on Inward Bound please send a message to info@inwardbound.com.

Please enclose a self-addressed, stamped envelope for reply or $1.00 to cover costs. If outside the U.S.A., please enclose an international postal reply coupon.

INNER PASSAGES

WILDERNESS,

HEALING,

AND THE

DISCOVERY

OF SELF

OUTER JOURNEYS

1998
LLEWELLYN PUBLICATIONS
ST. PAUL, MINNESOTA 55164-0383

FIRST EDITION
Second Printing, 1998

Cover design: Lisa Novak
Cover photo: Digital Stock Photography
Interior photos: Dave Cumes, M.D.
Author photo: Jonny Rozsa
Editing: Rosemary Wallner
Book design: Amy Rost

The illustration "A large-body experience" in chapter nine appears with the permission of J. D. Lewis Williams. The illustration "Num energy" in chapter nine appears with the permission of Dr. Aron D. Mazel. The schematic drawing "Needle and Thread" in chapter ten appears courtesy of Paul Cumes.

Library of Congress Cataloging In-Publication Data
Cumes, David, 1944–
    Inner passages, outer journeys: wilderness, healing, and the
discovery of self / David Cumes. —1st ed.
        p. cm.
    Includes bibliographical references.
    ISBN 1-56718-195-3 (pbk.)
    1. Spiritual life. 2. Nature—Religious aspects. I. Title.
BL435.C84   198
291.4—dc21   97-32122
                                                                CIP

PUBLISHER'S NOTE

Llewellyn Worldwide does not participate in, endorse, or have any authority or responsibility concerning private business transactions between our authors and the public. All mail addressed to the author is forwarded but the publisher cannot, unless specifically instructed by the author, give out an address or phone number.

Llewellyn Publications
A Division of Llewellyn Worldwide, Ltd.
P.O. Box 64383, Dept. K195-3
St. Paul, MN 55164-0383, U.S.A.

Printed in the United States of America.

⮑

I dedicate this book to Lila, Terry, Paul, and Romi,
who, even when they did not know it,
shared these experiences with me.

⮑

CONTENTS

ILLUSTRATIONS

TABLES

PREFACE AND ACKNOWLEDGMENTS

THIS BOOK ABOUT SELF-DISCOVERY IN wilderness is a pragmatic distillation of various sources of information on the transformational and healing qualities of nature. It is illustrated with personal anecdotes and is divided into three broad categories. The first concerns the relevance of the San hunter-gatherers of the Kalahari to our wilderness experience. The second highlights some important wisdom from wilderness and transpersonal psychology. The third deals with ancient mystical traditions and energy systems that can help us define a universal or core truth, which we can carry with us on our trek to realize Self. The principles elucidated apply as well to all those on any quest for self-actualization.

The multifaceted splendor of nature has the power to create what I have termed "wilderness rapture." This unique feeling occurs when we draw nearer to our higher self or inner being. The text explains how to facilitate this experience.

For the purpose of clarity, I found it necessary to make a clear demarcation between inner-directed and outer-directed experiences, between inward bound and outward bound, when they are not always readily distinguishable. The seeker's intention will determine whether the bias will be one way or the other. Those on the inward track may be forced to go outward because of a calamity or a crisis, and may find this enlightening. Conversely, their motivation may be primarily outward, yet there is a significant inner effect; exposure to the elements and the diverse polarities that abound in the wild can create profound shifts in awareness.

There are modern day hunters who appear outwardly directed and fixated on a trophy, but are mindful and meditative in their hunting techniques. There are mountaineers who seem totally resolute on attaining a peak, but who connect with their true being while climbing. No matter which it is—inward or outward, inner-directed or outer-directed, left or right, light or dark, feminine or masculine, sun or moon—we need to balance the opposites to achieve "wilderness rapture." When we focus on only one polarity we lose the magic and the ability to heal and restore ourselves.

To "achieve" is to be externally oriented; to attain deeper inner effects we need to let go of the attachment linked to accomplishing our objective. Goal orientation and rapture are mutually exclusive in the present moment. We begin with a purpose, but once the intention is set we need to disengage our craving for an explicit outcome. This is the crux between balancing inner and outer. The ability to be in harmony with oneself and with nature is embodied in the model of the San. Although the San have almost disappeared as hunter-gatherers, their unique consciousness and their relationship with the desert can be an inspiration to us when we go into the wilderness for healing.

I wish to gratefully acknowledge the San who gave me more than they could imagine; Adrienne Bates for all her support and encouragement and for making my time away from the practice feasible; Monica Fairall who inspired me to write my lecture into a book; and Bruce Dell who shared his bushman skills with me.

I also wish to thank Dr. Aron D. Mazel of the Natal Museum and J. David Lewis-Williams for permission to include their reproductions of tribal rock art, and Paul Cumes for providing the "Needle and Thread" schematic drawing and for other artistic input.

I treasure the many happy times with Black, Cecilana Gorfil, Steve and Penny Hochveld, and Jill Lieberman, who have been part of this book long before its inception.

Thanks to Carol Cumes who facilitated the early treks in Peru, to the staff at Llewellyn for their patience with my initial attempts to put these ideas on paper and for their skill; to editor Amy Rost for her talent and for being such a joy to work with; and to Susan Greenman for her help.

CHAPTER ONE

EARLY DAYS

AND THE

OUTER JOURNEY

WHEN I WAS GROWING UP in the late 1940s and 1950s, my psyche was small enough to require little space to develop. I lived in a house on a half acre in the suburbs of Johannesburg, and the garden became my first experience with nature. It seemed, at least at that time, big enough for my imagination.

My best friend, Cecil, and I used the garden to its full potential. It became deep, dark Africa, which we could explore to our heart's content. A huge mulberry tree held our rope swing and an apricot tree served as a tree house. When we tired of these, we disappeared behind the house into the lane that ran parallel to our street and separated us from the houses behind. The lane was full of bamboo—densely overgrown—and more than filled our imaginations with fantasies of wild Africa. It became the thick jungle we had seen in the Tarzan movies, and we easily fabricated predators, snakes, and the rest of the necessary components. Job, our Zulu cook, augmented the experience by teaching us how to make and throw spears. This area was big enough to captivate our interest and became our special retreat. Our play had free rein.

As we grew older and matured beyond playing in the garden, we enrolled in a youth movement that took us to other places farther afield. Our imaginations and the dimensions of our inner wilderness grew too, and the boundaries of our homes became inadequate to contain our adventures. The youth movement took us to farms in and around Johannesburg in the winter and to camps on the Indian Ocean in the summer.

The extent of our wilderness experience continued to expand. The camps usually involved a five-day hike that invariably was the high point of the three-week vacation. The hikes took us through pristine wilderness areas in the eastern Cape in and around Knysna, where indigenous forest and even a dozen or so Knysna elephants still existed. These animals added a special dimension to the trek, because, although we never saw those secretive beasts, we saw their impressive dung trails, which sparked our hopes for an elephant sighting. Knysna and the Tzitzikama Forest were my first experiences with pure wilderness, and I made a connection at a deep level.

Interspersed with these events were visits to my uncles' farms. My rich uncle, Aaron, had a magnificent subtropical farm in Pinetown, twenty miles from Durban. Along with chickens and cows there were banana plantations, mangos, litchis, and acres of space for me and my cousins to explore.

We entered the banana plantations with trepidation, because we were sure the area was teeming with deadly snakes—especially black and green mambas. My cousin Johnny had killed a six-foot rinkhals that he uncovered while pushing down a banana tree. The fact that there was real danger in this lush subtropical place added to the excitement. The monkeys down at the creek added to the adventure.

The farm also had a defunct swimming pool/dam full of frogs. We hunted there, although very soon it became clear that there was little pleasure to be gained from impaling a helpless frog. Eventually, we proved that cruelty to animals during one's early days often has little to do with later attitudes toward nature conservation.

My favorite uncle, Sam, bought a farm thirty miles south of Johannesburg. This was an ideal place for a boy, and I remember sitting around a Coleman power lantern while Sam designed his farm on the back of a cigarette box. Sam was full of exciting stories of the old Africa, and rapidly became my hero and role model. He had worked on the diamond mines and had ventured into different parts of South Africa in his younger years. He was never short of fascinating tales and was eager to share them. He always seemed to be happy and loved having people around him. I was lucky enough to see him realize his dream in the later years of his life, as this farm materialized from cigarette box cover to reality.

At Sam's farm I spent weekends and holidays shooting his guns, riding horses, and playing in the virgin veld around the farm. In those days leaving Johannesburg and driving to the farm was a special event. As we approached the farm I felt a sense of relief coupled with a feeling of excitement upon entering something new and fresh.

As I grew up, I felt a need to connect with the wild outdoors—at whatever level I perceived necessary at that time. Early on, the outdoors that appeared to be wild was not really wild at all, but it was sufficient for my psychic needs. When I was young, my exploration often was tentative. As I grew up, however, the need continued and the depth of my exploration intensified. I was fortunate to have many opportunities for this exploration so that, as my inner wilderness expanded, there was more than enough outer wilderness to connect with and to match it. Later on in life, I often wondered what it was that made me yearn to escape to wild areas.

Jane Hollister Wheelwright and her daughter, Linda Wheelwright Schmidt, discuss the phenomenon of bonding with nature in the formative years in their book *The Long Shore*. Their farm in central coastal California, when still wild, came to be symbolic of "the true self," whereas the outside world seemed representative of the ego, or the smaller self. The ranch became the source of power for them and in the absence of personal nurturing from parents, they turned to the farm as their resource. They found the mother archetype in Mother Nature. They noted that the earlier a child is imprinted with nature, the more likely the inherited primitive, psychological layer will predominate, allowing the child to cope with the power of what wilderness has to offer.

When I entered medical school, the time spent camping and trekking in the pristine wilderness more than made up for the grueling hours and the sometimes brutal training program. In fact, the time outdoors made the studying all worthwhile. My time in the wilderness was the Grail, or gift, that followed these severe years of initiation.

After receiving my medical degree, completing my internship, and spending a year abroad, I returned to South Africa and a rigorous five-year residency in general surgery. Besides the residency, I had another reason for returning to South Africa: I wanted to explore the Southern African outback so that if I ever left the country again I would know I had covered it intimately. I purchased a four-wheel-drive Jeep, a rare commodity in those days but one that gave me access to places I would otherwise have only dreamed about. While I was abroad, I had been struck by the lack of wilderness in England, the rest of Europe, and Israel, and realized I could never live permanently in a country that did not offer this outlet.

It felt good to be back in South Africa. The four-wheel-drive took me to the real wild Africa; Botswana and Mozambique had things to offer that one could not get in South Africa. The beaches of Mozambique were superlative and the wildlife of Botswana unparalleled. In between, I worked hard at becoming a proficient surgeon. I carefully balanced the two parts of my life in order not to burn out, and always had time to replenish myself in nature. I flip-flopped between two types of healing: the structured discipline of healing others with surgical techniques and my own holistic form of healing and restoration that occurred best in nature. As mentioned later in this book, there appeared to be two different types of energy use or attention involved: one that was restorative and the other that was depletive.

Although much of my energy in those early days of surgical training was outwardly directed, I learned a small truth about the inner journey into wilderness while spear fishing in Mozambique. I noticed that as soon as I had a spear gun in hand I saw nothing of the coral and experienced nothing of the underwater magnificence of the subtropical Indian Ocean. I became goal-oriented—my ego was at stake. I felt I needed to bring something back to camp for the pot. This was nonsense, because we had plenty of food. Later on that same trip, I stopped taking my gun and drifted among the coral reefs enjoying the freedom. If I had had the weapon with me, I would have either come back empty-handed and disappointed, or returned with a fish that may have paled by comparison to the size and number of those fish shot by the other more proficient skindivers. To eliminate this predicament and divest myself of ego, I divested myself of the spear gun.

The same appeared to be true of hunting, and I came to a similar conclusion on an expedition to a friend's farm in the far north. Four of us were trekking in the heat, hoping to find something for the pot. Cecil and I were novices; the other two were experienced hunters. One unfortunate antelope made itself visible that day, and Bayniss shot it in quick time. When we skinned the animal, we found it riddled with parasites, a depressing sight for Cecil and me, who had serious misgivings about the venture to begin with.

IN RETROSPECT, IT IS APPARENT how masculine a place Africa was. Everything required action and energy, and one was always too busy with little time for reflection. Maintaining the vehicle, finding one's way, setting up camp, filming, and fishing were the order of these days. It seemed that men often missed the essence of Africa's energy because they were so busy. The women, however, were different. Their behavior was more inclined toward a sense of being than a being of action. They were happy just to sit in a gorgeous place and enjoy it. We men sometimes became irritated with them.

The following example epitomized the outwardly directed experience of Africa. Some friends and I were in the middle of Chobe Game Reserve in northern Botswana in two four-wheel-drive Jeeps. I stopped to change a front tire after a flat and noticed that the wheel was loose. Graham, who owned the other Jeep, was a knowledgeable mechanic and felt that something in the bearing required tightening. He said we could tighten it that night in camp.

That night, in the middle of nowhere, we jacked up the front of the Jeep and stripped down the wheel. Graham neatly arranged all the parts in order, on a white towel. The overhaul was accomplished by the suboptimal lighting of a gas lamp. Deidre, Graham's wife, walked by after having just washed her face and saw the towel on the ground. She neglected to notice the parts neatly arranged on it and picked up the towel to wipe her face. We spent the rest of that night sifting the dirt for all the parts, putting them in order, and reassembling the wheel. The job was done by dawn, and Graham did not speak to Deidre that day.

Although I always felt that my friends and I were connecting with the essence of Africa on our trips, experiences like the one above highlighted the fact that much of the time we took our cognitive abilities—or left brains—and conventional behavior patterns with us into the wild. Sure the trip was different and refreshing, restorative and healing, but always outwardly so. We were men being boys again, recreating the same fantasy scenes Cecil and I had acted out so many times in our backyards. This time, however, the scene was real, something of which we always had dreamed. The bush was authentic and the animals were, too. Our trips as grown-ups were ways of going on a warrior's journeys in a physical way. We were conquering fears and mastering the outdoor skills. We had designed our own form of "Outward Bound."

Each time I completed a wilderness trip, something shifted within. I built up competence and increased self-esteem, self-concept, and possibly even some self-awareness—but I had no idea that there could be more beyond this. Sometimes, however, I sensed that better ways of being in the bush must be possible—even if it was not the intent to make a mystical encounter or connection with a greater part of my spirit.

I began by thinking that I could avoid the wheel-bearing incident and similar maintenance problems by placing as little between me and the wilderness as possible. The less there was to bring and support, the more likely I could connect with the pure essence of the African experience. It occurred to me that there might be other ways of experiencing wilderness more profoundly.

Sitting in a vehicle while viewing game, I was the one trapped and the animal was free. I took spectacular photographs because the smell and fumes of the vehicle disguised my presence. I found that the game in the different reserves became used to the vehicles and close sightings were common. Nevertheless, I felt separated from the experience by being confined to the four-wheel-drive.

To get rid of this feeling, I walked trails in the Umfolozi wilderness in Zululand and in the Kruger National Park. Here, my friends and I went out on trail with a qualified guide, armed with a rifle to protect us from predators. We did not see as many animals because they saw, heard, and smelled us first and made off long before we could get a sighting of them. Our human stench was no longer obscured by a metal box that emitted carbon monoxide and, therefore, close encounters with game were much less likely. Yet, I could get more easily into the essence of Africa, especially once I had seen my fill of the animals from a vehicle.

By this time, I had had marvelous experiences and photographs of game close up, and had witnessed some spectacular kills by lions. Having satisfied my need, it was enough just to walk in the bush and know the animals were there. I did not have to see them. Every now and then, they reminded us of their presence by their scat, their spoor, and their calls. I found myself relating to other fascinations in the bush, such as insects, plants, bushes and trees, sunsets, sounds and scents, and at night, the stars and the call of the bush. Animal sightings became a privilege rather than a prerogative. I had entered the next phase of my African outdoor education.

At the same time, I became introduced to the concept of a Land Rover-based wilderness trail. Here, a guide drove a group of people to a fixed camp with many luxuries—not as sophisticated as at home, but very innovative. Refrigeration kept beer and wine as well as meat cold and fresh, and there was even a hot shower at night.

The shower arrangement in the bush comprises a drum of hot water raised on a pulley, with a shower head and valve coming out of the bottom of the drum. There was always the exciting possibility that a lion or hyena might be prowling around, and could bite you in the rump. This thought added greatly to the adventure of the experience. The greatest danger, however, would be your instant demise if the rope broke or the knot slipped, dropping a ten-gallon drum full of hot water on your head.

The idea of the Land Rover-based trail is to have as much luxury as possible in the bush. But to my way of thinking, this type of trip takes people out of the wilderness experience. The alcohol flows at night, as do the jokes and stories. There is nothing wrong with this except that the atmosphere is the same in the local pub at home. You lose the essence of the African night unless you walk off on your own to experience it alone.

The next morning, a little hung over after one too many beers, the group jumps into the Land Rover and drives to a spot from which the wilderness trail proceeds. This type of experience is externally based and everyone is intent on identifying everything down to the last detail. Someone may be just about to get into the essence of communing with the African nature spirits when the guide whisks everyone back to camp in the Land Rover and offers another cold beer. This trip is enjoyable, relaxing, and fun, but it is a quantum leap away from another type of wilderness experience—one where there are no luxuries or alcohol to prevent you from connecting with your inner self in the bush. This latter experience of nature is different, more multifaceted, and mystical—you become part of the mantra and music of bush sounds.

⌒

THERE IS WISDOM IN JOHN Muir's statement: "Only by going alone in silence can one truly get into the heart of the wilderness. All other travel is mere dust, hotels and baggage and chatter."

Although I anticipated not seeing much wildlife when on foot in the bush, I have thus encountered some of my best sightings. As I become extremely relaxed and attuned, it is not difficult to slip into the so-called alpha state, which can be recognized on an electroencephalogram of the brain as a slower rhythm than the usual waking beta state of about thirty-two cycles per second. During normal consciousness we operate in beta, which is the fastest of all the normal rhythms recorded. The slower the brain wave activity, however, the more profound the state of altered consciousness. If you practice, you can go from beta to alpha to theta and finally to delta where the rate can be lower than four cycles per second. (Theta is a state well-known to accomplished meditators. The delta state is utilized by shamans in trance and advanced yogis, but without skill and experience in this rhythm, one is likely to fall asleep.)

In the alpha state (which is easy to induce), I am more likely able to approach animals closely on foot. Wildlife is exquisitely tuned into pheromones, which are extremely subtle scents released by different animals. Fear is a potent releaser of pheromones. If I am totally fearless in the bush and in the relaxed alpha state, animals tend to ignore my presence. If the wind is just right, I can get up very close.

On one occasion a group of us had just completed a five-day trek along the Inca trail into Machu Picchu. I entered the ruins and saw a llama among the magnificent Inca stonework. Without thinking much about it and being in a profound state of relaxation compatible with the alpha state, I approached and put my arms affectionately around the animal, giving it a welcome hug. The llama seemed to appreciate my warm greeting and did not object in the least. A nearby tourist, thinking this was an ideal opportunity for a unique photograph, approached the animal after I left and beckoned to his wife to take a picture of him, the llama, and the Inca shrine. As he came within a few inches of the llama, the beast spat in his face—something they are known to do when annoyed. I attribute this difference in reaction to a difference in mental state: the tourist in the normal beta and me in the alpha.

I have noticed this same reaction with elephants. The second I start to feel anxious and uncomfortable around these beasts, the animals' whole demeanor changes toward me. No doubt they are picking up on my fear, possibly by way of released pheromones.

Every now and then in South Africa there is a well-publicized snake-sitting competition. Some lunatic goes into a snake pit full of deadly serpents such as mambas and cobras for a hundred days or more. To remain in this pit of potential death, the person must be in an extremely relaxed, calm, meditative state and become one with the snakes.

⌣

WHEN I LEFT SOUTH AFRICA in 1975 I was beginning to appreciate the country, but had not been able to fully verbalize the kind of experience I was looking for. By the time I left South Africa, Rhodesia had become Zimbabwe and the Portuguese had pulled out of Mozambique. There were major changes on the subcontinent. I had qualified as a general surgeon and completed my residency in Johannesburg. I decided to immigrate to the United States to specialize in urology and was lucky to obtain a residency position at Stanford Medical Center.

My first two years at Stanford were dismal. I no longer had the outlet of the African wilderness that had rescued me so many times while I lived in Johannesburg and endured the months of surgical training. In South Africa, I always knew that when things got bad, I could take a week off, pack up my camping gear, jump into the Jeep, and head off into some remote region to recharge my batteries and restore my psyche. I came to realize that as beautiful as California was, it was hard to escape from crowds, bathrooms, gift stores, freeways, and sophistication. My knowledge of true American wilderness was scant and our kids were small. Backpacking into the California outback was not a possibility.

By now, I was done with my initiation phase into American medicine. I was on my way to becoming chief resident and fully enjoying the challenge of academic surgery. Somehow, wilderness and wildness were put on the back burner, and I was reconciled to not being in Africa anymore. Every now and then, I was reminded of an African scene and a strong nostalgia flowed back. My family and I made periodic trips back to South Africa to connect with old friends and family and try to recreate past experiences, but things never seemed quite the same. My move to California had put an end to my wilderness experiences as I knew them and had opened up a whole world of new non-wilderness possibilities.

For the first two years in Palo Alto, the move felt like a form of soul death to me, like I had lost a loved one. It had separated me from my inner self. The parting with Africa had been far more significant than I could have realized, and I had not yet learned to compensate for it by using the American wilderness.

All the energy I had spent trying to make it in the United States had changed me. I no longer had the same energy or life force; something was missing, and I did not know how to reconnect with it. I seemed to have lost a part of myself somewhere in the African veld. I could not convince myself that professional success was making me happy.

At the same time marital disharmony nearly culminated in a divorce. Many critical factors have been known to lead to personal growth and transformation, including severe illness, near-death experiences, psychedelics, mystical revelations, and loss of a job. I now fell into the one called loss of a loved one. The shock caused a huge shift in me, and I woke up to new possibilities. I undertook my own search to find that part of myself I thought was settled somewhere in the dust of Africa. I realized I had a Self, a soul, and that I was duty bound to find it.

I had started yoga exercises, and this trauma propelled me into a new dimension of the practice. I read extensively on alternative medicine and different spiritual pathways. I believed in the affirmation that "when you are ready, your teacher will appear." It came to me in the form of two yoga teachers in Santa Barbara, California, who ran an ashram on the top of San Marcos Pass, fifteen minutes from my home.

I recognized how powerful a tool yoga became for me. It lifted my spirits and enabled me to enter an inner dimension, which felt extremely comfortable. I began to recognize that this was similar to the sense of peace, harmony, and oneness I had experienced in the South African bush country. The combination of peculiar body movements and weird breathing techniques had a significant impact on me. This was not something you could read in a textbook—you had to feel it.

Yoga became the tool for accessing my Self or "atman," as it was intended to. I had read about yoga and how the practice of simple *asanas* or postures could change your thinking process, how you behaved, and how you ate. I once thought this unlikely, but it started happening automatically. My body tuned into its inner needs, and I followed.

It seemed that many things Western science could not explain simply worked. I stopped trying to discount these beneficial effects and became more of a pragmatic scientist, looking for experiential rather than theoretical knowledge. I became open to the Zen concept of "beginner's mind."

Kabir's words seemed to say it best:

> *Kabir talks only about what he has lived through.*
> *If you have not lived through something, it is not true.*

Right about this time I had an unusual dream—not a dream as such, but rather a voice that said to me in my sleep state: "It is better to experience the learning, than to learn the experience." I try as much as I can to remember this advice.

Following a sixteen-day intensive with my two friends in their magnificent yoga center overlooking Santa Barbara's Channel Islands, Ganga (one of my friends) turned to me and said, "Now you have your M.D. degree—Master of your own Destiny." I felt that what he said was true; I was on the path back to my true self, and this path led back to my roots in Africa.

As a child and at school, I had been enthralled with the tales of the San people, or Bushmen, of the Kalahari. One of my dreams had been to stay with them for an extended period on my own. I saw this dream as the easiest route to finding my lost Self; I expected to find the greatest spiritual truth in the Kalahari. It was this primal, primeval, and primitive experience that proved to be the sophisticated lesson I needed to learn which way my path would turn. I have no doubt that it was this stay in the Kalahari that led me to wilderness healing and enabled me to work with the medicinal power of nature. The Bushmen were to become for me the ultimate model to emulate in wilderness.

⟳

FURTHER READING

Bly, Robert. *The Kabir Book*. Boston: Beacon Press, 1977.

Browning, Peter. *John Muir in His Own Words*. Lafayette, California: Great West Books, 1988.

CHAPTER TWO

THE SAN

HUNTER-

GATHERERS:

THE ULTIMATE

WILDERNESS

MASTERS

The spirit of man is nomad, his blood Bedouin, and love is the Aboriginal tracker on the faded desert spoor of his lost self; and so I came to live my life not by conscious plan or prearranged design but as someone following the flight of a bird.

Laurens Van der Post

DURING THE PRESENT TIME OF rapid growth and political change in South Africa, little has been said about the original indigenous people of Southern Africa, the San. A native North American elder once said that if one is born in a country, the ancestral spirits of that place gradually seep into your psyche and, whether you know it or not, have an effect. I cannot help but think that this is the case insofar as my upbringing in South Africa was concerned. The spirits of the subcontinent, San and others, have had a profound influence on my soul.

The Bushmen, or San, are one of the last hunter-gatherers of Africa. In the late 1980s, it was estimated that there were about 60,000 San living in the Kalahari and less than 1,000 living as their ancestors did in an almost Stone Age existence. There are even fewer living this way today.

The San have attracted various groups of people for different reasons. Anthropologists see them as a link to long lost Stone Age cultures. Naturalists and hunters admire them for their extraordinary expertise in the bush. Those of a more mystical inclination are fascinated with their oneness with the Kalahari's fauna and flora, a connection that has enabled them to survive for centuries in a wasteless desert most other peoples have avoided. Through this, the San seem to have remained free from the trappings and problems of more sophisticated societies.

As a student at school, I had grown up with tales of the San. I learned how they could not be tamed and that the northerly migration of the whites and the southerly migration of the Bantu pushed the San farther and farther into the interior of Southern Africa. Stories abounded of their cunning as hunters and trackers, their botanical and medicinal skills, their delicate rock art, and their bravery. Their desire to be free was paramount; it was said that if you imprisoned a San he would soon will himself to death. The San people are so much in the present moment that a captive San is unable to conceive of a time in the future when things might be different and he could be free. The San also have significant mystical and paranormal powers; it is possible that, like master yogis, they are able to choose the time when they wish to pass over onto the other side to join their ancestors.

⤶

I N 1987 I TOOK MY first extended trip to visit the Kalahari San. On this occasion I spent time with them alone, which enabled me to connect with them on a very personal level. (Since then I have been back several times with family and friends, and each time have noted an increasing erosion of the old way of life. The essence of the early San is fading and needs to be remembered and preserved before it is lost, more especially for those with an abiding passion for the wild.)

Before 1987, my contact with the San had been cursory; passing through, taking photographs, buying a few of their wares. On this occasion, however, I had arranged with a knowledgeable South African, Izak Barnard, to join a small group of travelers in the southeast of Botswana on a visit to a band of Kua San.

With Barnard and the group, the San showed us how to track, trap, and find water, bulbs, roots, tubers, and other *veldkos* (the Afrikaans word for "food from the veld or bush"). Other skills, such as fire making, were included. The days with the group swept by. After a week, Barnard headed back to Johannesburg with his group and left me with a four-wheel-drive Landcruiser and a steel trunk full of provisions. I had a small tent and a tarpaulin to shade myself from the brutal southern sun. A local Tswana, called

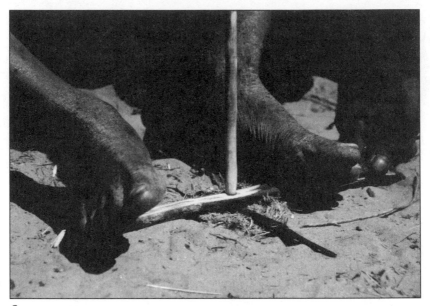

SAN FIRECRAFT.

Loose Boy, was to act as my guide and interpreter. Although he spoke little English, he had worked on the mines in Johannesburg and spoke Afrikaans, so I was able to converse with him. His deficiency in English was epitomized by his name, which came from the fact that he was blind in one eye. Because he had "loosed" it, he became Loose Boy.

Any doubts about what was to happen were dispelled quickly, as the San medicine man already had cast the bones and told me I was going to have a good stay. Previously our group, led by Barnard, had camped in some proximity to their whereabouts, and the San had come from surrounding areas to squat and visit. We had counted a total of 170 next to our encampment. They now had drifted back to their respective homes. Four San men, along with Loose Boy, immediately adopted me; these five were to stay with me for the duration of my visit.

Titigaai, Koti, Latlecha, and Tsumu were to be my hosts and Loose Boy the go-between. These four were also the most desirable men of their clan, and most of the time five young San women completed our group and added a feminine dimension.

The San selected a good spot for my camp, somewhat shaded by thorn trees and about 300 yards from their own encampment. Rapidly they set about helping me. In no time at all the tent was up, thorns and scrub cleared, and, most important of all, the small tarpaulin was strung cleverly between trees to offer maximum shade from the Kalahari sun. Already I had experienced this in the preceding week when temperatures hit 120 degrees Fahrenheit in the shade, and all one could do was find the best thorn tree available and limit activity to zero.

The San are very intelligent and the way I had seen them work in the last week was testimony enough. Teachers of San children have been quick to point out their above average intelligence and abilities. I found this a big factor in communication, for even without Loose Boy they seemed to know exactly what I wanted or was trying to get at most of the time.

Physically, the San are quite different from other South African peoples. They are short of stature and have copper-colored skin, peppercorn hair,

A SAN HUNTER ENJOYS A MYSTIC MOMENT.

The San people have delicate facial features, slanting eyes, and high cheekbones.

and delicate facial features. They have slanting eyes and high cheek bones with more of a Mongoloid than a Negroid appearance. This has led to speculation as to the origin of these original indigenous people of Southern Africa, whose origins go back at least 40,000 years.

The women often are exquisite and have a characteristic sign of steatopygia, an excess of fat accumulation in the buttocks, so that they project somewhat behind them. Buttocks are the most important part of the anatomy when it comes to sex appeal and, except on special occasions, are always covered. Some of these features are disappearing as the San mix with their Bantu neighbors. Already this was apparent in a few members of the group.

The women provide most of the food by foraging, and I was privileged to go out with them on many occasions. They are outstanding botanists and, while walking at quite a pace, could discern subtle changes in the shapeless Kalahari scrub denoting something edible. Out would come the

A SAN MOTHER GATHERING FROM EARTH MOTHER.

The San women use their extraordinary foraging ability to provide most of the food for their tribe.

ubiquitous digging stick, and within seconds a delectable morsel would be thrown into the skin bag.

Many of the roots, bulbs, and tubers are quite deep underground and have to be uncovered a foot or more down. (It is only deep under the surface of the earth that they can acquire enough moisture in which to grow.) San women moving through the bush are a formidable harvesting machine. Even toward the end of my stay, when I was familiar with the different plants for that particular season, I missed 90 percent of what they found. On occasion I proudly dug up something that resembled the plants they were foraging, only to be greeted with laughter and the word *poysen,* one of the few English words with which they were familiar. One to two hours later and five skin bags full, they would return to camp with enough food for all.

The San own little and share everything, although with the advent of interested whites like myself, who bring gifts and pay for services rendered, this too is changing. I was filled with admiration when embarking with the men for a veld trip—all they had with them were a bow, a quiver of arrows, a digging stick, a fire stick, and a sipping straw to suck water out of hollow trees or from sipwells in the sand. With these simple implements and their incredible knowledge of the desert, they could survive indefinitely, whereas I would barely last a few days. If they had left me in this featureless wasteland, I doubt I would have been able to find my way back to camp. Few landmarks exist in the Kalahari, and one thorn tree looks like another to the uninitiated. To the San, however, each area has its own tale to tell. Their knowledge extended many miles beyond their camp, and when we took the Landcruiser miles to the north, they were just as familiar with the terrain.

It is nothing for a San to walk fifty miles to visit friends. Boarding schools had a problem with San children running away to the friendly fires of home, finding plenty to eat along the way back.

These San were extremely egalitarian. They had no chief or leader and everyone—male and female—had a say in the activities of the group. Certain members were known for their extraordinary skills of hunting or healing, but this did not confer on them any additional privileges. Egomaniacal attitudes were not part of San behavior. The men could take more than one wife but, because of the rigors of providing, the group

A SAN HUNTER WITH HIS BACKPACK.

The pack contains only a bow, arrows, a digging stick, a fire stick, and a sipping straw, yet has everything the hunter needs to survive in the desert.

A SIPPING STRAW DEMONSTRATION.

One of their few possessions, the San use the straw to suck water out of hollow trees or from sipwells in the sand.

mostly was monogamous. San women have been known to have two husbands, but this is rare. Women do not hunt but provide most of the food by foraging. The men too were excellent foragers and frequently brought back food after a day in the veld. The women rarely danced but controlled the energy of the dancing by their chanting and clapping. Most of the healers were men, but women could also be healers and often were the most powerful and respected.

Children had a unique role and were thoroughly spoiled, in our terms. When a child picked up a musical instrument, allowance was the rule, no matter how distracting the noise. I rarely saw a child have a request refused, and no San adult could bear to hear a child cry. If I offered a piece of candy to one of the adults, it was nothing for a child to snatch it out of my hands, to the laughter of the adult who had thus been deprived. Once I came across a young boy beating his mother furiously with a stick. Her response was to laugh, protect herself from the blows and defuse the whole situation, so that she ended up cuddling him. She never once raised her voice or struck him back in this profound demonstration of unconditional love. The Kalahari desert is a cruel enough teacher, and the environment outside of home holds enough to teach youngsters to be responsible adults. Even amongst the adults, an unconditional positive regard for others seemed to be routine and it was difficult to find judgmental attitudes among the group.

✑

M Y DAYS WITH THE SAN were full, and there was much to learn. I realized that it took years to become an accomplished hunter-gatherer, and all I could achieve in my short visit was a deep appreciation of the knowledge and abilities of the San.

We went out twice a day, in early morning and late afternoon. The San knew I was interested in learning their skills, and they were eager to teach them. Rope making was essential, because without it one could not make a bow or snare. This basic skill was one of the easiest to learn, but it took me hours to do what took them a few minutes. Their rope was made from a small fibrous-like plant called *Gwi* (*Sanserveria*, also called mother-in-law's tongue), which was easily found in that particular area. The rope was extremely strong, and even a cord of string made from it was difficult to break.

There was a well several miles from the first camp so that water was not an issue for the group. Water containers of plastic bottles have replaced empty ostrich egg shells, and it was an acceptable daily chore to walk five miles to fill them. Still, they were grateful for the intermittent use of the Landcruiser, which could carry a forty-four-gallon drum.

Water is like a drug to the San, and wells put in by the Botswana government are among the factors that have put an end to their nomadic way of life. It is so much easier to turn on a faucet than to go and dig for tubers and look for Tsama melons, even if it means a walk of five miles or more. So except for a few purists—like the group I was to meet later—the San tend to settle in close proximity to a well. Nevertheless, the skills for finding water still remain and the San are adept in their use. It is likely that future generations growing up with water faucets will lose these skills. Dependency on the well meant that women and men had to forage further and further afield for food and firewood. The San way of life had been predicated on their being transient, but the presence of a well became a strong deterrent to their nomadic way of life.

One day while out in the veld miles from camp, there was a dramatic thunderstorm. It proved to be one of the most exhilarating experiences of the trip. Rain poured down on our almost naked bodies in the middle of the Kalahari desert in mid-summer. It was a singular experience, and we got back soaked and happy. In my mind's eye I still can see us sprinting over the desert with the rain coming down and lightning and thunder all around. Rain is rare in the Kalahari, but when it occurs, water collection is an easy matter until the sun emerges to quickly dry up the desert. Hollow trees fill readily and are protected from rapid evaporation by their shade.

The next day we left early with decorated ostrich egg shells with grass stoppers for corks. These were filled with water from hollowed out tree trunks, using hollow reeds to suck the water up and spit it carefully back into the shell. These natural wells were covered meticulously with a log or branch to prevent animals from drinking and polluting it. The Kalahari has no natural water and it rains infrequently. Before the advent of the well these people did not have water, yet adapted happily to the environment. With all my trivial complaints, this realization was quite an eye opener.

Later we traveled thirty miles north in the Landcruiser to another small settlement. These people had no access to the well and were living much the same as their ancestors had for generations. They showed us how they dug for the tuber they called *Baiee*, grated it with a sharp stick, and delivered the juice inside. To this they added one or two different plants to take away the bitterness and catalyze the release of more water, because they could squeeze an excessive volume from a modest amount of the shavings. This group of people wasted nothing; they used the fiber's residue to scrub and clean themselves. These people had not seen water for several weeks. When we gave them the half gallon we had, I was fascinated to see them pass it around and drink without anyone, including the children, clamoring for a share. At the end some went without, again with no complaint. Later we were to return to spend time with this group.

The camp I had been staying with was relatively prosperous and clearly influenced by the Tswana, the indigenous Bantu people (of which Loose Boy was a member) living all around. This second group, however, was quite different. Here the Kalahari still felt pristine, as did the San, and it seemed as if this small band of people was holding out on moving to the well, intent on maintaining the old way of life.

Many pressures threaten the San way of life besides the introduction of water on tap. Huge cattle ranches have appeared with fences that both limit game migration and inhibit the nomadic pattern of the San. Cattle overgrazing is a problem with regard to the destruction of natural habitat and food to forage. Game preserves and hunting areas have been demarcated and the San are no longer welcome, even though their hunting needs are small and do not affect the ecology. The San, as hunter-gatherers, are slowly disappearing because it is easier for them to assimilate with the Tswana around them. The elders of the clan in the camp we visited seemed to realize this and had opted to hold out as long as possible.

Hunting with these groups of San had become a rare event, because little large game remained in the area. Meat, however, was not in short supply because of the Sans' ingenious ability. They concentrated on the

HUNTERS CAREFULLY SETTING THEIR TRAPS.

The traps are designed for smaller animals, especially duiker, steenbok, and guinea fowl.

trapping of smaller animals, especially the delicate duiker and steenbok, which still were prolific in the area. They also caught guinea fowl, which were also numerous. Watching them set a trap reminded me of a surgical exercise. They paid minute attention to detail, and trapping had become a work of practical art. More astounding was the knowledge of the animals, as they "became" that animal, chatting away to each other and discussing all aspects of behavior and how best to set the trap. It seemed uncanny that in this vast expanse of desert they would be able to eat meat just because one buck placed one foot in a six-inch diameter spot somewhere in the Kalahari. Although after two weeks I could set a sloppy trap, it was clear that it took a lifetime to learn where to set it.

Skinning of the animal was done quickly and efficiently on a table of broken branches in the sand. Nothing was wasted and the delicacies—the heart, kidneys, and liver—were wrapped in the stomach and cooked in an ash oven or pot. These were the privileges of the hunter, and the rest was shared. In times of drought the San squeezed the liquid from the stomach contents for a drink; survival in the Kalahari laid esthetics aside.

Farther north it still was possible to hunt gemsbok and hartebeest, two larger antelope. This was not practical on foot for the San in terms of their energy equation. The San would not expend more energy than they could get back from the exercise because, with water and food being so critical, walking so far to hunt could become a life or death situation. However, with the use of the Landcruiser, they were eager to see if we could bring back a gemsbok. The medicine man cast the bones and informed us that if we went in a particular direction the next day we would see them. He was right.

That day we went to look for *poysen* for the arrows. The poisonous grub of the diamphidia beetle can be found a foot away from the bush *commifora*, and it was here that we spent several hours digging. It was hard to imagine how the first San discovered that the innards of this grub were deadly when in contact with the blood stream. Perhaps it came to one of them in an altered state of consciousness during the "trance dance." The poison is a neurotoxin that causes paralysis with a curare-like effect. The time it takes to kill depends on the size and weight of the prey and the San have been known to track a large wounded animal for a day or more.

To prepare the arrows, the San wind sinew around the metal shaft of the arrowhead and smear the poison onto it; they take great care not to put any poison on the point of the arrow. A mere scratch could be fatal, and there is no antidote. It is easy to understand why the quiver is solid and made from a specialized piece of hollow bark. This is one activity the children are not allowed to share.

The San are small people, and their bows and arrows are toy-like. They do not rely on a fatal shot from afar, as their incredible tracking ability and stealth allow them a shot from up close. The poison takes care of the rest. The wooden body of the arrow is arranged cleverly to drop away from the poisoned metal shaft, which remains stuck in the flesh so the animal cannot dislodge it by rubbing up against a tree. The poison is deactivated by cooking and also by gastric juice.

With the arrows poisoned, we were ready for the next day's hunt. We awoke early and, after an hour's drive past our most northerly camp, we were in a region with numerous gemsbok and hartebeest spoor, along with countless others that the San easily distinguished. They could tell how many animals had passed by, which were male and female, their size and approximate time of arrival. Even if a track looked relatively recent, they knew that the animal had too much of a head start to be worth following; and this happened frequently. They laughed tolerantly at me when I suggested we go after the "fresh" ones.

Then came a different response. I must have been driving twenty miles an hour when they banged on the roof of the vehicle, commanding me to stop. They had spotted very fresh spoor and excitedly we made off into the bush on foot, the San gliding through like dolphins in the ocean and me coming up behind. They seemed to know instinctively when they were getting close, because the scrub was thick and it was hard to see. Koti spotted them first and beckoned for me to come around so I could get them in view. They were barely fifty yards away, but as I was lining up my camera they trotted off out of range. The San seemed more interested in my recording the gemsbok on film instead of shooting one for the pot. In times of need, however, it might have been different.

On our way back, a Botswana official spotted us. He questioned me closely as to what I was doing in this area, and asked if I had a permit to take photographs. We said nothing of the proposed hunt, although the San later told me they were entitled to hunt in the area. The official was particularly perturbed by the South African registration of my Landcruiser, but was happy to learn I was an American citizen. He cautioned me that in the future I should travel in a locally registered vehicle or run the risk of getting lynched. Politics could not have been further from my mind until then, and I was pleased that we did not have the additional burden of a gemsbok carcass in the back of the pickup to explain.

$\backsim$

T HE NIGHTS IN THE KALAHARI were extraordinary, and everyone seemed to welcome the release from the heat of the day. The best times for me were the days spent in the more northerly camp far away from the humanmade well. Here, the Kalahari felt as it must have for millennia, and the small San encampment seemed untainted by the twentieth century. Furthermore, the six of us were accompanied by the same five women, and we were all visitors to the clan. We camped out together and slept around the fire on the earth under the incredible southern skies. The Southern Cross comforted me that I was back in Southern Africa.

These San had only rudimentary shelters in which they rarely slept but kept mainly for their meager belongings. One night when it rained I moved into the small shelter with the rest of the group. I was struck by the fact that the shelter appeared to be almost a living organism—so much noise and rustling was going on in the wall's brush, sticks, and grass. The walls became a haven for the fauna of the Kalahari, and every now and then had to be burned down and reconstructed.

When evening came, the *veldkos* was roasted in the ashes and eaten with cornmeal and some Western food from my supply. After that there would be singing and dancing, and I would sit under the startling Kalahari sky, listening. San music has a haunting sound and is different from anything else I have ever heard; it easily can propel a person into an altered state of consciousness. Dancing usually accompanied the singing, which changed to more of a chant with clapping accompanied by the swishing

A HUT UNDER CONSTRUCTION.
The walls of the rudimentary shelter will be covered with brush, sticks, and grass.

sounds of ankle rattles the men wrapped around their legs. Given the right energy and enough time at the dance, the San are able to fall into a trance.

The San dance is an art that enables a healer to leave his or her body and do battle with ancestral spirits for the restoration of the health of the patient. It also is known as the "Little Death," because the dancer is in danger of not returning to the body and has to be carefully watched. Trance dancers have been known to do remarkable things with fire, including putting their heads in flames without suffering burns. They are known for their psychic and healing abilities, and many Africans prefer to see a San healer than be treated by their own medicine person. Many whites in the Kalahari testify to being cured by a San healer after Western medicine failed them. I did not witness a trance dance with this particular group of San, and when I asked about it they evaded the question. (Barnard, who knew this group intimately, told me that in earlier times he had seen them trance.) On a later visit I was to see the power of this spirit flight in the northwestern part of Botswana, where the Kung San live.

❧

O N MY LAST NIGHT THERE was a spectacular sunset and a huge full
moon on the opposite horizon—the sun and the moon, or the *Ha*
and *Tha* of Hatha, signifying balance. These unique people seemed to have
found the balance we others lack in our modern society, and it disturbs me
how some people find the San intriguing because of their "primitive"
lifestyle. In many ways they are far more sophisticated than so-called "modern" cultures. Without much effort, they attained the higher principles so
often quoted by the mystics of Eastern religions—joy and living totally in
the present moment, lack of judgmental attitudes, unconditional love, and
being in the flow of nature and the cosmos.

It also appeared that the only tool they had that enabled them to reach
this enlightened state was the purity of their relationship with wilderness.
They had no esoteric techniques such as meditation or yoga and could not
read or write. For this reason I began to believe that nature alone may be
one of the most powerful spiritual forces available for personal growth, if
accessed in the right way. If we are to derive this benefit as Westerners, we
need to have as little as possible between us and the wild. The more we separate ourselves from Mother Nature, the more diluted the effect.

The Kua San depicted the Mother Earth as a pregnant woman created
by the great spirit Bisi. The huge belly of the woman (as one of the San
drew for me) was ruptured, giving forth all the animals of the veld. The
skin of the woman then became the crust of the Mother Earth, whom the
San treat with the greatest respect. The concepts of Gaia and Deep Ecology
that we are only now beginning to embrace are second nature to the San.
The purpose of my visit to the San initially had more to do with learning
the superb bushcraft or "hard" skills they had mastered in their brutal environment. With time, however, I became far more interested and impressed
with their group interaction, or "soft" skills, as well as their spirituality.

These qualities seemed to arise from their austere way of life, which had
been self-imposed for generations. Rather than assimilate with the Bantu
or on white farms, the San chose freedom in the depths of the Kalahari.
Unfortunately, cattle ranching and the four-wheel drive have put an end to

THE KUA SAN CREATION MYTH.

Mother Earth (bottom left) is depicted as a pregnant woman giving forth all the animals of the veld. The skin of the woman then became the crust of the earth. One of the San drew this sketch in the author's diary.

their unique, unfettered way of life. Change has now overtaken the San, and some have been overwhelmed by the temptations of modern consumerism and alcohol. They are well aware of some of the commodities that could make life easier. But with each acquisition they become a little less free, without understanding that, by gaining something material, they are actually losing something far more precious.

The change in their way of life is most obvious in the alterations in their dwellings. They now have simulated the Tswana way of building and are separated from each other by small huts with doors on them, and fences of acacia thorn stand between the homes. Previously, the San slept together on the earth, next to the fire. But as they acquired more possessions, they developed fear about who might dispossess them. San healers who once trance danced in an altruistic, holistic fashion for the sake of the clan, now charged for services rendered.

There is nothing special about the San psyche. They are the same as Westerners and, if anything, more prone to the temptations of materialism. What has been unique was their habitat and connection with the earth and cosmos, and this birthright is being taken away from them. Moreover, the San have tasted the fruit of a consumer society and have been seduced by its power. The attraction of "things" has overwhelmed them, and the ego sense of the San has changed. The social structure that kept everybody humble and egalitarian with little emphasis on ego has fallen away, and with this depletion, their spiritual life continues to deteriorate. Nevertheless, small groups of San continue their ancient healing traditions; some San have learned to live in two worlds, reconnecting with the wilderness as the need arises.

We can use the San model to reconnect with that primeval hunter-gatherer part of ourselves that resides deep in our psyche and was operative and functional for eons. By doing so, and by keeping as little between us and the wilderness as possible—as the San have done—we can tap into a different spiritual dimension in wilderness. We can learn from their egalitarianism and humility because Eastern philosophy teaches that ego is the greatest obstacle in reaching our inner being. The healing dance of the San is a powerful way of harmonizing the group, connecting with the ancestral spirits and the Great Spirit, and healing sick members of the clan. The San believe that sickness or imbalance resides in all of us, but only becomes ill-ness or disease in some. It is only with regular rebalancing with the use of the trance dance that health and equanimity can best be retained or restored in the group. At a more basic level, it is when we reconnect with that hunter-gatherer part of ourselves that we can understand this balance.

The San and other hunter-gatherers close to the earth are the ideal examples for those of us wishing to formulate our own wilderness prac-tice. Few of us will ever learn what it feels like to be a hunter-gatherer, to be so connected to wilderness that one needs it to survive. The true hunter-gatherer relates to nature beyond the five senses and lives in a psy-chospiritual dimension that we can appreciate but rarely experience. How-ever, we can hunt and gather in the supermarket, fill our backpacks, and walk into the wilderness for a week or more. This simple act can have pro-found healing consequences and help us connect with a part of ourselves that we may have lost. The essence of this inner journey is in keeping it simple and having the minimum of material possessions between our-selves and the wilderness. Carefully scrutinize anything that separates us from nature, whether it be a horse and its care or a video camera. It is best to venture forth on foot with a backpack, because it is then unlikely that anything redundant will be carried.

⤳

EVENTUALLY IT CAME TIME TO leave the Kalahari and the San. I struck camp with the help of my friends who wished to ride with me to the trading store some twenty miles away. The sun was rising and Loose Boy came to me and pointed to a square object on the horizon. It was about twice the size of the morning star. He asked me what I thought it was, but my focus was now on getting back to Johannesburg on my own in the Landcruiser, and I did not pay much attention. He walked away tolerantly. Enroute to the trading store, we stopped to visit Loose Boy's home and family. Everyone pointed directly above us to a shining object. Now it was impossible to ignore, and Loose Boy said in Afrikaans, "I know what this is. It is people from another place." A shiver went up my spine. If there is anything amiss in this environment, these people will notice it immediately. Loose Boy volunteered that he had seen similar objects before, but usually not so clearly. We watched the object, which seemed to hover motionless above us for fifteen minutes.

As we drove off to the trading store, I looked out of my side window intermittently. The lateral view looked more balloon-shaped, with a central pod extending down and two shorter pods on either side. It appeared to move sideways, and whenever I looked out of the window it was in the same position. This continued for the duration of the drive to the trading store; we never lost sight of it on the right side of the vehicle. It continued to hover over the trading store while I chatted to the owners and filled the Landcruiser with gasoline.

I said good-bye to my friends and drove off toward Gaberones, with the UFO still in sight. Unfortunately, my attention was taken up by intermittent stalling and overheating of the Landcruiser, which necessitated frequent stops and diverted my attention from the object. It drifted off toward the horizon into the clouds and out of sight. Up until that point I had an overwhelming sensation it had been following me. No sooner had it left than the Landcruiser's overheating seemed to self-correct.

When I returned to Johannesburg, I consulted the National Institute of Telecommunications Research and was told the only thing that resembled my description of the object was a French research balloon. The expert hastened to mention that these had not been in operation for many years. (Some years later—by which time I had begun to discredit and rationalize the occurrence—a physicist patient of mine who had observed and studied UFOs, told me that the problem I had experienced with the Landcruiser was a common event resulting from disturbance of the ignition system of the vehicle by radiation emanating from the UFO's power source.)

I returned to California confused as to how I was to proceed with my inner life, but realized that wilderness would have much to do with it. I continued to delve into various aspects of esoteric interest including shamanism, meditation, yoga, and alternative healing techniques, particularly Ayurveda, the ancient Indian system of healing.

I was very familiar with wilderness medicine insofar as it could help me or a fellow traveler get out of sticky health situations in the bush. Now I became most interested in a different kind of "wilderness medicine"—healing or restoration resulting from the special qualities of wilderness itself—and found that few people were using wilderness as therapy for healing at the level of one's inner being. I gleaned little information from the few books that talked to the subject. The wilderness psychology literature was full of data, but the closest I could get to the word *healing* was the term *restorative.* The psychology information seemed limited because the authors could only report what could be measured objectively and most of what happened in wilderness could not be put down in words. I decided that my role was to study the mechanisms creating the transcendence and healing that has been labeled "the wilderness effect" and facilitate this in the context of venturing into wilderness.

Martin Buber said, "All men have access to God, but each man has a different access." My access to God and my higher self was to be through the medium of wilderness. My experience in the Kalahari had enabled me to connect with the San consciousness and return with a different awareness. Of all the things that impressed me about the San, their lack of ego struck me the most. It was this more than anything that seemed to confer on them a sense of wholeness. They appeared to be in much closer contact with their inner being than many of the sophisticated New Age people I had encountered over the years in California.

Laurens Van der Post who was raised by a San nanny had a deep appreciation of what the hunter-gatherer may hold for us as we approach the new millennium. Carl Jung, Abraham Maslow, and Eastern philosophies have said the search for the true self (or real self or higher self) is at the core of all human motivation. Whether we know it or not, we are searching for this connection and the drive is always present, even if subconscious. The higher self is that God-like part of ourselves mentioned in the Old Testament or to a Christian way of thinking is called the soul. In yoga texts, it is the Atman. In order to reach our inner being or higher self, we must work through the ego and recognize its limitations.

The ego and persona, "the mask," are connected intimately. The persona is who we think we really are and depends on status symbols and material possessions to support it, such as degrees, titles, money, the house we live in, the car we drive, the colleges our kids attend. According to Eastern philosophy, in order to be spiritually awakened, ego and persona need to know that there is a larger picture lying beyond. Hence, the term *transpersonal*, as in *transpersonal psychology*, in which one must go beyond the persona or ego to the transcendent. It is in the place beyond ego that the wilderness effect occurs.

As we shall see in chapter nine, ego is closely connected to a sense of power and is centered around the third chakra. This energy center in our body described in yoga and Buddhist texts is situated in the solar plexus area and helps us make our way in the world. Our personality is centered around the ego and it is a vital part of our development and makeup. However, in order to become self-realized or spiritually enlightened, the ego must subordinate itself to the higher self.

The San manage to reach these higher dimensions not by any esoteric practice but by their intrinsic connection with nature alone and by exposure to the multifaceted properties she possesses. Their trance dance, where they travel out-of-body by opening their hearts and transcending ego, is a powerful demonstration of this (see chapter nine).

The true self does not need anything to support it, but stands alone. Activities that are inner-directed tend to shift us toward our true self. These are done for their own sake and have no ulterior motive. This higher self is the place of inner peace, calm, harmony, and at oneness. The little self, or ego, is the place of suffering. Nothing satisfies ego, there is always more money or fame to acquire and bigger and better things to collect. We all believe if we only had just that little bit more we would be happy. Of course, when we get it we are not. If we spend extended periods in nature, with the right intention, it is easy to let go of ego and allow the higher self to emerge. When this occurs, we appreciate a sense of wholeness, unity, wonder, and healing at the deepest level of our existence.

There are many forms of inner-directed activity, and if we were Zen masters every function of our lives would be a meditation. The Zen concept of mindfulness can be a miracle but it is difficult for most Westerners to achieve. Wilderness is a natural and powerful catalyst for the inward journey and is diverse and varied enough to cater to anyone. Nature herself can be a natural meditation—"leave-no-trace" or minimum-impact camping are forms of mindfulness practice. Solitude may be part of the experience and if one adds to this any number of inner-directed techniques such as meditation, breath work, ceremony, and ritual, the power of the wild outdoors can be amplified tremendously.

Wilderness is another way to connect with our inner being and the closer we can get to the model of the hunter-gatherer the more powerful the wilderness effect. Experiencing nature is non-denominational and is a tool for transcending ego and reaching for a deeper reality.

∽

Further Reading

Lee, Richard B. *The Dobe Kung*. New York: CBS College Publishing/Saunders College Publishing, 1984.

Thomas, Elizabeth Marshall. *The Harmless People*. Capetown, South Africa: Africa South Paperbacks, 1988.

Van der Post, Laurens. *The Lost World of the Kalahari*. Middlesex, Great Britain: Harmonsworth, 1958.

Van der Post, Laurens and Jane Taylor. *Testament to the Bushmen*. London: Rainbird Publishing Group, 1984.

CHAPTER THREE

INNER PASSAGE OR OUTER JOURNEY: WHAT'S IT TO BE?

I only went out for a walk and finally decided to stay until sundown, for going out I discovered was actually going in.

John Muir

O N A RECENT TREK IN the Drakensburg Mountains, I accompanied a group of trail leaders from the Wilderness Leadership School in South Africa. We shared the experiences of our early youth that led us to choose outdoor careers or orientations. All the trail guides in the group, experienced in leading trails for the school, had some early childhood background with nature.

These were people who had chosen wilderness as a career, unlike myself who had chosen it as a hobby and personal sanctuary. Nevertheless, when I look back, it was apparent that I had connected deeply with nature in my formative years on family farms. Later when I started medical school, my Uncle Sam's farm remained a retreat for me, but a weekend's sojourn no longer seemed sufficient. Although surrounded by miles of wild veld, it was not enough. Once I obtained my driver's license, I began to make forays further afield to different parts of South Africa. Soon the horizons, in terms of South Africa's wilderness, began to seem limited and I ventured into Mozambique, Botswana, Zimbabwe, and Namibia. It was here I could easily find the old wild Africa. After completing medical school, a four-wheel-drive Jeep made even the most remote places accessible.

My initial connection with the soul of Africa was at my uncles' farms, and I involved myself in a youth movement from the age of ten until shortly before I completed medical school. Twice yearly there were camps and seminars, and these served to intensify my connection with nature because they were held in outdoor retreats. As my responsibilities grew, my need intensified to reconnect with these places that generated so much peace. Medical school holidays found me replenishing myself in the outback, and after I graduated I sought sanctuaries even more remote. Each grueling milestone of schooling or training was punctuated by a retreat somewhere to restore myself.

Although I connected with a sense of calm, of oneness and inner peace, my trips also were outwardly directed. The four-wheel-drive, the camping gear, the tools, and necessary spare parts (you never seem to have the one that was required for the breakdown) were all part of the scene. Other facets, such as spearguns for shooting fish and a movie camera to record the adventures, placed me outside the inner experience. Invariably some trauma would occur to necessitate the use of those faculties I was trying so desperately to rehabilitate. For example, the four-wheel-drive was not necessarily enough to compensate for bad judgment that resulted in my becoming stuck in a river.

Wilderness medicine and the use of innovative techniques to resolve the inevitable mishaps also contributed to the daily activities. It was possible to be as busy in wilderness as at home, employing the usual skills in a holiday situation. In my younger days, however, it seemed I had boundless energy, enough to spread around in every possible direction. Everything seemed fun and challenging and—insofar as it occurred in a new environment and under unique circumstances—one could say there were significant restorative components to this type of work.

Rachel Kaplan and Stephen Kaplan discuss William James' definition of attention. James divided attention into two parts: voluntary or involuntary. Kaplan points out that these terms are somewhat confusing and labels them more accurately as directed or non-directed attention. Directed, or voluntary, attention is used in day-to-day living. It requires much effort because there is a need to eliminate competing stimuli and input. With overuse, the capacity for directed attention becomes diminished and leads to mental fatigue and burnout, with decreased functioning and a lowered tolerance for frustration. This frequently manifests as selfishness, aggressiveness, decreased patience and sensitivity to others, and a lessening of the ability to control one's reactions. Sleep has limitations in decreasing mental fatigue. A truly restorative experience is associated with non-directed attention, which evokes interest, curiosity, fascination, and harmony with the surroundings.

Nature is a preferred environment that is compatible for most people and as such has tremendous potential for restoration. Kaplan adds that in order to be preferred, however, it must feel safe to the individual who can then explore without concern about taking unnecessary risks. Environments that are preferred and safe are less likely to result in directed attention, do not deplete our cognitive capacity, and are more restorative. The "soft" fascinations found here occur in the space of sunsets, scenery, sights, sounds, and smells. They seduce our senses and create attraction, enchantment, and even rapture. Non-directed attention is also evoked during the use of "soft" skills such as group interaction, meditation, singing, drumming, and ceremony. Just because one is in nature or the wilderness does not make it inevitable that the experience will be restorative. We need to recognize whether we are using directed or non-directed attention (see Table 1).

DIRECTED VERSUS NON-DIRECTED ATTENTION

Directed Attention	Non-directed Attention
Requires much effort.	Effortless.
Demands we shut out competing stimuli.	Creates interest, curiosity, fascination.
With time, the ability to concentrate decreases.	Captures attention. No need to concentrate.
Left-brain activity.	Right-brain activity.
Attention directed externally.	Directed inward.
Causes mental fatigue, burn out, stress, decreased tolerance for frustration.	Mental relaxation, faculties restored, healing.

TABLE 1.

I once completed a month's wilderness course in Kenya with the National Outdoor Leadership School (NOLS), one of the largest and most respected outdoor schools in North America and the world. Its philosophy is based on minimum-impact camping and giving participants enough skills in wilderness so they can remain comfortable, warm, dry, well-fed, and safe. The thrust of its commitment is on wilderness leadership.

Those weeks spent in Kenya National Park were extremely busy. We navigated, learned different cooking and baking techniques, and attended classes on high altitude sickness, hypothermia, back country first aid, evacuation, and more. In school, the wilderness became the classroom rather than a place to restore our psyches. Little time was afforded to connecting with the magnificence of what surrounded us, but that was a given, considering the NOLS philosophy. This was to teach outdoor "hard" skills, not to connect one with the transcendent in nature. This is entirely appropriate because if one cannot be safe in the wild, the transcendent becomes unimportant, and it would not be desirable to encounter it in the form of a near death experience. Nevertheless, it is illustrative of directed attention in wilderness and transferring everyday cognitive abilities to the wilderness situation.

Goal-oriented behavior in wilderness can lead to the same thing. If one's sole objective is to "bag a peak," run a river, or make a destination within a certain time frame, one can enter into a technical exercise not connected with the uniqueness of nature.

On another occasion a friend and I decided to go backpacking in the Wind River mountains in Wyoming. The two of us had trekked a lot together and were both more interested in the inner aspects of the wilderness experience. Although it was never discussed, we wanted this to be a large part of the journey. The hike was preceded by a wilderness conference in Lander, Wyoming, which is the NOLS headquarters. Before we set out, we talked to a group of NOLS instructors about our route. One of the men who was familiar with the area suggested we go up Wind River Peak. We told him we only had four days, to which he replied, "You can make it in four days." We did make it, but the trip became goal-oriented and four days was not enough to get there and back and connect with the "Winds" at the same time. The trail bordered on an endurance trip, which did not give us time to connect at a deeper level. Had we bumped into our informant after the journey, and if he had asked if we "made it," we would have been slightly embarrassed to say "No, but we did stop and smell the roses."

Outward Bound runs courses with the idea of self-mastery in mind. The philosophy of this school is to increase the technical difficulty of various exercises where success leads to a sense of mastery in the wilderness situation, which can be reflected as a metaphor into real life. Outward Bound, like NOLS, is ostensibly an outwardly directed experience and many of the activities invoke the use of directed attention. However, at the end of the training there usually is a forty-eight-hour solo, which many candidates often report as the most powerful aspect of the trip. Here, the students are offered the great opportunity to connect with soft fascinations and go inward when left on their own in the wild. Outward Bound may imply that participants are "bound to go outward," leaving little room for the inward except possibly at the time of the solo. *Outward* includes the main objectives of the organization, namely increasing self-mastery, self-concept, and self-esteem; this self being distinct from the higher or true self encountered in the inner journey in that it is centered around the ego. Only when we reach beyond ego do we become self-aware and cognizant of a "bigger" self with deeper meaning. Unfortunately, Western conditioning is such that we believe that only things centered around the ego are valuable.

Outward Bound historically has been through three distinct models of operation over the years. The first was called the "Mountains Speak for Themselves." The groups were taken into wilderness and nature was allowed to perform its magic without facilitation. This is the type of experience I was familiar with in my earlier days of trekking. The South African bush spoke for itself in the context of an expected type of social interaction, where even the mention of group interaction or meditation would be looked at with disdain. This type of hike was distinctly macho in orientation and a softer approach would have been regarded as wimpy. There was little appreciation that an inner-directed orientation could lead to a more profound experience.

One July, some years ago, my son Paul and I took a canoeing trip down the Zambezi River. This is not something one can easily do on one's own, so we joined a group with a river guide. The group was small and pleasant enough. As I was there with Paul, who was then seventeen, an inward journey into wilderness was not my primary goal. This was more of an initiation ceremony for him, taking him back to the subcontinent of his birth. (Paul had been born in Johannesburg shortly before we emigrated to the United States.) Ultimately, it became an initiation for us both when we sank our canoe in the crocodile-infested waters and, on another occasion, ran into a bank, face to face with a Cape buffalo three feet away. Fortunately, the buffalo was more startled than we were and ran off into the reeds, and the Zambezi crocodiles were not particularly hungry that day.

Each day we stopped on the banks of the river to enjoy our lunch, and I took this opportunity to walk off into the bush to meditate. This must have disturbed Jim, our intrepid leader, who probably did not want to be held responsible for my being eaten by a predator.

One day while we were enjoying lunch on the river bank, Jim related a story about Bob, his apprentice river guide. He related how Bob would disappear over the lunch break, much as I had been doing, and no one would know where he had gone. On one occasion Jim decided to follow him and, while hiding behind a tree, noticed that Bob was doing some strange things. He found the macho Zimbabwean touching, feeling, and talking to the trees, bushes, shrubs, and plants. It was clear to me that Bob had been in a state of wilderness reverie, but to Jim and the rest of the group this was an occasion for snickering.

At the end of the river runs, Bob and his group would beach their canoes close to the Mozambique border where a four-wheel-drive would meet them for the return to the town of Kariba. After driving a short distance with the group, Bob would stop the vehicle, say good-bye to everyone, and walk off into the bush on his own with very few provisions. The walk back to Kariba was a two- or three-day hike through thick bushveld, flat savanna-type terrain covered with scrub, and acacia thorn trees abounding in wildlife, including large predators.

Jim continued to illustrate Bob's "odd" behavior as it deviated from the group's. Finally, he told us how one day Bob had presented himself downstream from the Victoria Falls, asking if he could run the rapids in one of the kayaks. The white water in this part of the world is formidable, and on being asked by the professional kayakers whether he knew how to kayak, Bob answered affirmatively.

It was apparent to all after he climbed into the kayak that Bob had never before run rapids. He spent most of the time submerged upside down in the Zambezi, and eventually was jettisoned from the kayak and swam the river the rest of the way. As he emerged at the other end, he excitedly told those who had arrived to resuscitate him that this was one of the best things he had ever done. Again, this was described by Jim in such a way as to demean Bob, rather than to recognize him for the pure wilderness man he was.

To me, the story epitomizes a problem with adventure trekking today. There is tremendous social pressure to do what the group does and not to appear at all different or strange. The result is merely a continuation of the same behaviors occurring at home and in the workplace. Even on the Zambezi it becomes difficult to step out of everyday reality into the surrounding world of wonder, and people tend to maintain their regular daily habits. We hesitate to be alone and spend even a little time away from the group to contemplate and meditate. In spite of this, the wilderness continues to work its magic even if in a somewhat diluted form, because "the mountains do speak for themselves!"

The second model that Outward Bound developed was called "Outward Bound Plus." The same familiar skills courses were applied, but group interaction complemented each exercise and it was found that this model was more successful than the first.

The third and most recent model is the Metaphoric Model where a particular exercise is used as a metaphor and becomes psychologically identical to a real life situation, or "isomorphic." The experience is designed to be successful, facilitating self-mastery and self-esteem, and the achievement can be applied to true circumstances in everyday life with a resulting improvement in managing a given challenge.

Outward Bound's courses are extremely successful in increasing self-mastery, self-esteem, and self-concept, and its trips often lead to peak or transcendent experiences in nature. Nevertheless, the emphasis of these schools—whether NOLS, Outward Bound, or others—is on utilizing directed attention in much the same way one would use it for any training technique. The power of nature is such that it still has a transcendental effect although these may only be considered incidental bonuses arising out of the curriculum.

⤴

THE BRAIN HAS BEEN SIMPLISTICALLY divided into two halves: left and right. The left side often is referred to as more masculine: cognitive, intellectual, logical, and analytical. The right is more feminine and is intuitive, symbolic, compassionate, creative, and empathetic; it is compatible with non-directed attention and the inner-directed wilderness experience. It seems appropriate to label this the "inward bound journey." The left brain, however, feels more at home in the hard skills, outward journeys of NOLS or Outward Bound and being cognitive operates with directed attention.

In my early days in Africa, my forays were more outwardly bound. Nevertheless, no deadlines or schedules existed and there was time for contemplation or just "being." It was all wonderful. The outward activity appealed to my very left-brain orientation and when, almost unconsciously I would slip into a right-brain mode, I was replenishing my psyche and having a whole brain experience. Now that I am older, the psychological need for the inward experience has supervened. I am less anxious for physical challenges, especially when contrived. There is a difference between accomplishing a difficult river crossing if the option is turning back, and doing a technical exercise because the group leader says you should. There is a difference between crossing a high mountain pass to continue your route, and scaling a rock face just because it's there. Physical feats that have purpose and meaning are more likely to be fulfilling than ego-oriented tasks; Kaplan affirms that people like to do tasks that "matter." I am happy just to be in the wilderness and allow it to offer up its challenges spontaneously; there are enough of those. This is the more so because my work in medicine is so cognitive, demanding, and outward that when I do get away from it I need all the restoration that I can get in a short space of time.

But in those early days I did not understand any of this, and I just had a good time. As the Kabbalists (Jewish mystics) well knew, something changes after the age of forty, and there is a shift in the psyche. It was for this reason that no scholar was allowed to begin the study of Jewish mysticism (Kabbalah) until the age of forty. One's energy resources decline around that time of life, directing what energy is available in another way, to go inward.

Many of those people I have been with on trails already had accomplished a certain self-mastery in their lives. They had done all the right things and achieved all that society demanded of them. In spite of adhering to the book of rules, there is little self-satisfaction and inner peace following this attainment of materialistic success. One has gained the carrot at the end of the stick and found that in consuming it there is not much pleasure. Thus, many of us turn inward and look for completion by connecting with that deeper part of ourselves.

⤿

O N MY FORTIETH BIRTHDAY I TOOK my first trip to Peru. On this shamanic journey it was apparent that the women in the group made a strong connection with the mountain energies of Peru—a place very different from Africa. Everything seemed softer, not only the scenery, but also the people. Although South American culture is quite macho, there seems to be a matriarchal influence, and the machismo paled by comparison to what I was familiar with in South Africa.

Just as psychologists and neurologists could divide brain functions into left and right, masculine and feminine, cognitive and intuitive, I could divide my understanding of certain geographical and physical facts, or geomancy, into similar contexts. Peru became the place of the feminine, the intuitive, creative, empathetic, and compassionate. Africa remained a place that was more masculine, cognitive, harsh, and goal-oriented. Peru was the *Ida nadi* of the yoga chakra system: the cool, pale, blue, moon, or feminine energy. Africa was the *Pingala nadi*: the hot, red, sun or masculine energy. Women seemed to change in Peru. They made significant life adjustments and did strange things; this was born out on my subsequent visits to Peru.

The females seemed to tap into a different dimension of themselves not always comfortable for their male counterparts.

When I thought about it more carefully in the context of Peruvian wilderness, it was much easier to just "be" in the Andes. Cognitive knowledge was not significant to the experience. The fascination that abounded was "soft" and led to more profound contemplative and meditative states of mind. Add to this the mysteries of the ancient civilization, about which little is known, and you had an ideal model for fantasy, imagination, and going inward. You could make up your own theory on the significance of different Inca ruins, because no one seemed to know otherwise. It seemed a relief to just wander aimlessly around Machu Picchu and meditate on the meaning of different structures. Most theories about the place appear to be conjecture, and those offered up by the shamans seem just as plausible as those given by the most sophisticated archeologist. There was no doubt that even to the cognitive, male psyche, Peru was a place of magic and fascination. The imagination could run wild and meditations could be profound. Non-directed attention abounded.

⌒

I RETURNED REPEATEDLY TO SOUTH Africa to renew my African and possibly male "fix," now with my children, who I wanted to introduce to the land of their origins. On these return journeys, the contrast between Africa and Peru seemed more stark in my mind. The bushveld demanded certain cognitive skills to survive, and the men could remain on automatic pilot and transfer directly from their work-a-day world into the African outback. One could get very technical about how to be in the bushveld, and the cliché "You don't have to live like a barbarian to enjoy the wilderness" was taken seriously. All this led to great ingenuity, toys, and gadgets when it came to camping.

By this stage, however, I had moved completely away from this externally directed camping experience with all its accouterments. I was interested in wilderness backpacking with as little as possible between myself and the bushveld except for an experienced guide with a gun, which was reassuring and necessary in the wilds of Africa. In spite of this, the experience remained "masculine." There was a certain coded behavior and toughness required. One was bombarded by countless things that needed identification and explanation. One could begin with big game and move on from there.

Africa is so rich that you would be lucky to know all there was to know about just the ungulates in one lifetime. After obtaining a working knowledge of larger and smaller animals, one could graduate to the finer points of learning about spoor (tracks). To reach a level of ability of reading spoor that approximated that of a San Bushman required many years of dirt work. A Bushman, white or black, can tell the type of animal, approximate size, time of arrival, sex, and much more by just glancing at a few tracks.

Having touched on tracking, one can go on to birds, their calls, and their mating habits. From there it is on to insects, spiders, scorpions, reptiles, and finally—if you live long enough—you can enter into the world of African flora and medicinal plants. This plethora of information inspires the left brain and requires directed attention. You can tap regularly into an external experience using all of your faculties to gain as much knowledge as possible. The bushveld is replete with people using binoculars and bird lists, ticking off the various birds they have seen in the course of a trip.

There is often a critical point at which a soft fascination becomes an interesting project requiring the use of directed attention.

One time I took a horse trail in the western part of the Okavango swamps in Botswana, accompanied by my two sons and a few old friends. One of them, Dave, was an avid birder and liked to pull out a list of birds at the end of the day so he could add everything he had seen in the past twenty-four hours. P. J. and his wife, who ran the horse trail, had seen it all and knew most birds intimately. P. J. had brought a small boat along so we could traverse the swamps and do some fishing. One day we all went out except for Dave, who was late in arriving and literally missed the boat.

We headed up one of the waterways in the crystal clear water of the swamps. There were lilies all around and African Jacanas were prolific, walking with great agility across the lily leaves. We decided to play a trick on Dave, and I asked P. J. for the names of three of the rarest birds ever seen in the area. Dave was an accomplished birder and would no doubt be impressed by us having seen such a collection. When we returned, he was waiting for us on the banks of the river. When he asked us what we had seen, P. J.—very matter of factly, with a straight face—rattled off the names of three rare birds. Although good-natured about it, Dave was clearly upset. These three birds would not complement his bird list that night.

It is easy to take oneself out of the purer essences of the wilderness experience. A camera can become a powerful distraction for the inward journey in nature, and the wilderness can be experienced purely through the eyes of the lens. On my first trip to Peru, my video camera became a convenient way of taking myself away from the shamanic ceremony at hand. In recording it I was not participating, and when I later showed the video to friends I presented the phenomenon as something bizarre but interesting, and clearly outside my framework of thinking. I did not wish to compromise my image as a medical scientist and in this way protected myself from any mystical experiences that my intellect did not want to confront.

Most women are much better than men at detaching themselves from the compulsion to name everything. One friend of mine said she does not care what kind of bird it is or what name it has or what it looks like in the breeding season: she can just enjoy it for what it is. Naturally, it is an impossible demand for someone who is not familiar with all that the African bush has to offer not to be sucked into the miracle of its complexity and want to know intellectually what is going on.

It may be best for the uninitiated, especially those traveling from abroad, to divide their African experience into two components. The first is a cognitive one in which as much as possible is seen and learned of the wildlife. The camera is an important part of this component. To this, however, should be added a five-day (at least) wilderness backpacking trip where one can detach completely from the goal of seeing anything in particular. The trailist can just "be" in wilderness and "be" happy to know that the birds and animals are there, whether they present themselves or not. Whatever does present itself is a gift, whatever fails to appear is not a disappointment. It can be sufficient tuning into the sights, sounds, and smells of the bushveld, identifying the spoor and listening to the bird calls.

Most people find it difficult to have an inner experience in the African bush because there is so much to learn. Having an inner experience requires walking a fine line between directed and non-directed attention with emphasis on the latter. The ego yearns for knowledge as a way of demonstrating power and has to be subverted to gain an inner experience. Non-directed attention is a challenge for most Westerners, especially in the company of a group hungry for information.

Even an attempt to meditate in the bush can be fraught with difficulty, because one's level of awareness usually is outer-directed just in case a hyena happens to come along. If one takes a watch around the campfire at night, many things present themselves, including animal sounds and the occasional sighting of a predator through the light of a flashlight. One is responsible not only for oneself, but for the group as well, and the level of protective awareness is more significant. It would be shirking one's duty to go inward—a sleeping companion might suffer the consequences. Naturally, there are mountains and deserts in Africa as well where there are no predators to divert attention and where one can contemplate in peace. Nevertheless, when in Africa the behavior is more patriarchal and macho, and that attitude prevails.

I was reminded of this on a recent visit to Johannesburg. An old friend picked me up for lunch and asked if I wanted to drive. When I said no, she reminded me that this was unusual, because most South African men still were not used to being driven by a female. It struck me at the time that if I tried to solicit interest for a wilderness trail into the bush where the more intuitive feminine aspects of the journey would be stressed, I probably would not attract many male participants. If the group is composed of a significant number of South African males, the bias invariably drifts toward an external orientation because that is the way of the culture.

I was also approached one evening in Johannesburg by an ornithologist after presenting this material to a group of wilderness enthusiasts. He remarked that it was interesting how cognitive and left-brained my delivery was in order to talk about something that was more intuitive and right-brained. The message was clear: we need both, and the magic occurs by achieving a balance between the two without becoming attached to either one.

⚭

WHEN I STARTED TO THINK about inwardly bound journeys for personal transformation, it occurred to me that for these reasons Peru, rather than Africa, was an easier place to facilitate the experience. I have no in-depth experience of other places in the world, but I am certain that there are many mountainous areas such as the Rockies, the Himalayas, and others that lend themselves just as well to the Peru-type of experience. Similarly, a jungle type of encounter either in India or the Amazon might tend to dictate a more externally directed journey.

There are, however, wilderness men and women who are so familiar with their habitat and the relevant skills that they do not need to be so attentive externally because being in the bush or the wild is second nature to them. Behavior in the external and cognitive world of Africa or the Amazon becomes automatic, and they easily switch into the internal and intuitive at any time they choose.

Tom Brown, a North American wilderness man, runs a survival school in New Jersey and has written extensively on Native North American traditions of hunting and gathering. He has said when someone develops the skill of a hunter-gatherer that person is able to enter into a different psycho-spiritual space, which those who have not reached this level of expertise cannot understand.

This is clearly so with the San of the Kalahari. They have mastered the hard skills and live in a different reality augmented by their closeness to nature and the cosmos. They are more able to use paranormal powers, or "the third eye" or "sixth sense" described in Eastern cultures. These people are using whole-brain activity to the maximum and can move freely between the two worlds of the external and internal, due to their exquisite expertise in the Kalahari desert. If one is fortunate enough to be with these skilled individuals, the external is taken care of by them, and one is more able to drift into the internal part of the experience. Naturally, being alone in this predicament could well result in a survival type of situation where all one's energies were externally directed. But with the help of wilderness masters such as these, it is easy to gain an internal experience because they are in control and the cognitive side of the brain can be put on hold.

A woman once approached me after a talk I gave and said, "Do I have this right? Do you run groups for women in Peru and for men in Africa?" Nothing could be further from the truth, but it helps to illustrate the point that gender is not the issue here. There are many women in the African outback who are tuned into the masculine experience of the left brain just as there are many men who go to Peru to tune into the feminine side of themselves.

Before embarking on any wilderness experience one must ask, "Why am I doing this?" Intention is obviously key here and the saying, "If you don't know where you're going, any road will take you there," is true. If the intention is an inward, healing, life-sustaining encounter with nature, the journey must be structured differently. Outer experiences are well and good, and it is possible to spend many enjoyable days identifying animals and their spoor and checking out different birds. Even when primarily in the external mode, one can still slip into the internal unconsciously and have a profound encounter with the higher self. For the inner journey, however, we require a different emphasis.

The leader and group will determine the type of experience. If the goal is externally directed, the group will be also. If bird lists are the order of the day, then the inner dimensions will suffer. If alcohol flows around the campfire at night, the experience will shift. If there is a time restraint that causes the group to hurry, performance orientation will supervene. If photography is paramount, the wilderness experience can occur through the camera lens. A wilderness leader who recognizes wilderness as a special place or sanctuary, affords it the deference it deserves, and gives people the space they need to go inward is rare. This unusual attitude will be conveyed to the rest of the party and the emphasis on the journey will change. Furthermore, it is likely that this type of adventure will be more restorative to the psyche.

Africa is full of skilled guides who are externally oriented, except for a few unique individuals. Few organizations stress the spiritual side in wilderness, and it is difficult to find groups pursuing the inward journey. The Wilderness Leadership School in South Africa is an exception. In the

United States, conventional outdoor schools and adventure tours do not cater to this venture and one must search the New Age magazines for sojourns into nature such as shamanism, yoga retreats, and vision quests. It is more difficult to find groups geared toward inner-directed wilderness backpacking, canoeing, or horse trekking experiences.

The criteria for an inward journey into wilderness should include a clear objective of the trip itself. The guide should have this in mind and be experienced in using different techniques to create the process.

Ideally the trip itself should be in pristine wilderness where there are few or no signs of human activity, and there should be as little as possible separating the trailist from wilderness. It is most desirable to approximate the San or any hunter-gatherer model so we remain closely connected with Mother Earth and the cosmos with as little technology as possible. It is the model of the hunter-gatherer that we can best use to facilitate and amplify our own inner wilderness experience. Even a horse that requires some care can interfere with the purity of the encounter.

In third world countries it is usually possible to find people who willingly help in payment for their services. They provide assistance for everyday needs and allow you to maximize your retreat. A unique inward journey should not result in an endurance test so that nature may offer up her hazards spontaneously. The trip leaders should possess all the hard skills necessary to keep the group warm, dry, comfortable, and well-fed. Some people have a natural resistance to contemplation and meditation, and the guide should allow generous space to those who wish to go inward. There should be enough quality time to enable this, as well as to allow some meaningful form of group interaction. Goal orientation and time restraints must be minimized to permit the true inner experience.

Backpacking and canoeing lend themselves best to a pure encounter with wilderness but horses, although a convenience, require care. Supportive help in the way of handlers are helpful in releasing the traveler from distracting responsibilities. Logistics of the trip are less important than the intent of the group and the skill of the guide.

It is not for us to evaluate anyone's relationship with wilderness. There are profoundly spiritual people who connect with nature in different ways, from hunting to ascending awesome peaks. It does not matter how each individual designs his or her own experience as long as it is fulfilling to the traveler and the wild outdoors does not suffer the consequences.

～

Further Reading

Bacon, Stephen. *The Conscious Use of Metaphor in Outward Bound.* Denver: Colorado Outward Bound School, 1983.

Kaplan, Rachel and Stephen Kaplan. *The Experience of Nature: A Psychological Perspective.* New York: Cambridge University Press, 1989.

Wheelwright, Jane Hollister and Lynda Wheelwright Schmidt. *The Long Shore: A Psychological Experience of the Wilderness.* San Francisco: Sierra Club Books, 1991.

CHAPTER FOUR

A MODEL

FOR HEALING

IN NATURE

Everything I have achieved in my own life, I owe to the wilderness experience. I have seen countless other lives molded and changed by encounters with wilderness: in most cases, only a few days in the wilderness atmosphere has been enough to change a life of despair into one of hope.

Dr. Ian C. Player

FROM 1986 ONWARD I BEGAN to explore anything about alternative healing I could get my hands on. I delved into subjects that seemed interesting, ranging from shamanism to acupuncture. It was clear that all these techniques worked, but what I also knew was that their effectiveness was uncertain. Many cases, all anecdotal, were cited of dramatic cures with methods unacceptable to mainstream medicine. There were no studies to show how they stood up to Western techniques, but what was impressive was that they sometimes worked where modern medicine failed. That was not to say that overall the results were better, but only that in some instances alternative treatments were more successful. I was looking for another way to express myself as a healer, but could not find the right kind of expression. I did not have the time or energy to restudy another system, such as Chinese medicine, homeopathy, or Ayurveda, and my passion lay in wilderness.

I did, however, change the way I related to my patients. I became more open and encouraged them to try different techniques in addition to the allopathic regimes I was recommending. I recommended visualization, meditation, yoga, special diets, and acupuncture. I came to realize that the healing I performed was occurring on a more superficial level. Frequently I was treating the effect rather than the root cause. I also came to realize that for the latter the patient would have to go deeper. In fact, there could be no real healing until they connected with their true or higher self at one level or another. It was only in an encounter with this "self" that an appreciation of one's truth would arise, and only if one became attuned to this would deeper healing occur. This might require painful lifestyle changes, but there was no shortcut to self-balance and health.

My personal practice gradually evolved into three aspects: Hatha yoga, meditation, and wilderness. Because I am a physical person, Hatha yoga became an integral part of my day. I realized that if much time passed without it, I would cease to function as well, with my frustration tolerance declining rapidly. I found the moving meditation of yoga to be a powerful ally in coping with the stressful demands of my surgical practice.

One day, while adjusting to the effects of high altitude on my first morning at 11,000 feet in Peru, a sense of knowing or a small voice crept into my consciousness as I rested on the bed. It said, "You need to translate your life into your physical body. This is your route to inner peace." The maximum amount of balance for me occurs in wilderness. It is here that I am in touch with my inner being in a more profound way and the wilderness requires a more physical experience.

Subsequently my lifestyle crystallized into wilderness sojourns every few months, with yoga and meditation practice in between to help maintain my equanimity. Essentially, I tapped into ways of going inward that worked for me. I knew there were other ways and I tried them to good effect, but yoga, meditation, and wilderness were the ones that fitted me best. I wove them around my medical practice, which most of the time was an intellectual, external activity, and the overall balance seemed to work. Whenever I found myself off-center I could understand what was happening—the inner life was suffering at the expense of the outer. I would then tap back into my Bushman consciousness and return to the wilderness to reset my thermostat. This not only gave me tranquillity but made me a more effective allopathic physician on my return.

What also was apparent was that wilderness seemed more powerful than yoga or meditation. The inner peace and harmony after a week away in nature lasted several weeks, and only then would start to dwindle. The effect of a regular meditation and yoga practice was much more short-lived, and if I skipped more than twenty-four hours I noticed a subtle change in my tolerance. There was something more restorative about going back to nature than anything else I could use to replenish myself.

Body, mind, and spirit were integrated by numerous factors, many of which were hard to define. Wilderness was a multi-disciplinary approach to burnout. It was the ramifications of these "disciplines" that intrigued me, as well as the mechanism that made one feel so whole while in wilderness. Yoga and meditation were tools to go inward, and an extended retreat using these techniques might have the same power as a similar nature retreat. In wilderness, however, if one avoided falling into the trap of the external, everything around seemed to facilitate the inward journey of healing.

It was in this context that I started looking for answers as to what was operating in the so-called wilderness effect. Wilderness was to become my non-allopathic healing technique, another way to do my work, but now at another level of the true self, both for myself and others.

There is no good term in wilderness psychology for the inner effect of nature on the psyche. For the sake of discussion, I call it "wilderness rapture."

⌐∽

M ANY PEOPLE HAVE SAID THAT wilderness cannot bear the brunt of all the healing that has become necessary in the face of the catastrophic changes in our society. It is easy to understand how we all would like to leave the wilderness pristine and exclusively for the few. But as more people tap its benefits, we can only hope that we can expand the boundaries of the wilderness to accommodate them. The way to protect it may be to allow more people to experience the wilderness power, because the ultimate conservationists are likely to have had a profound inner journey into wilderness themselves.

The new discipline of echopsychology suggests that because of the toxicity of modern-day society, any psychotherapy that does not address the way in which we live is bound to fail. We must evaluate the health status not only of ourselves but also of our environment and our culture. We all cannot return to the wilderness, but connecting with nature and our more primitive roots in some small way is a useful start.

There are numerous ways to experience the wild, as evidenced by the many outdoor companies catering to wilderness adventure. All of these, if run responsibly, have merit. But often the training that participants receive in external skills is done with little connection with the environment around them. The wilderness is used as a convenient classroom for expertise, and access to its deeper mysteries is unlikely to occur. Little time is left to connect with the magnificence that surrounds the students, and although it is omnipresent and hard to ignore, it can be difficult to "be" in, because being busy is the order of the day. In spite of this, wilderness works its effect and can lead to the well-described entity of re-entry depression. The depth of this despair is often a reflection of the balance and harmony created by nature, contrasted with the dismal prospect of returning to those catastrophes of life we had left behind when we first entered the healing magic of the wild.

I vividly recall one of our group on our last night of a wilderness skills course with the National Outdoor Leadership School (NOLS) in Mount Kenya National Park. We camped at the ranger station on our way out of the park. The group member was in a state of near panic trying to look for a little piece of pristine wilderness in the environment of the campsite, but she couldn't find any. We were now out of the experience, away from the sacred space. The integration phase and re-entry depression had begun. The inner power of the preceding weeks in pure wilderness became more apparent, in spite of the fact we had been on a skills course with an outwardly directed orientation.

There is little likelihood that the inward-bound wilderness experience can ever be scientifically evaluated, because much of what we are trying to analyze borders on the spiritual and is not easily measurable. This book makes little attempt to be scientific. The emphasis is on the inner journey into wilderness, and no excuses are made for the fact that we are trying to appreciate our higher self in the process.

It seems that if there is one unifying factor among all the confusion of what does and does not create the wilderness effect, wilderness rapture, or the healing, it is that connection with the higher self. This is what is driving us whether we know it or not. Just as holistic healing of a disease must ultimately begin with reconciling with the higher self and eliminating whatever is not true to it, relating to wilderness on an inner level depends on our connecting with our higher selves while using wilderness as the medium. All the rest is commentary and will have tremendous individual variation depending on our genetic makeup, present life situation, culture, religion, conditioning, education, and so on. We cannot hope to find a model that fits all, any more than we can hope to find a belief that fits all. We can, however, find an approach using basic spiritual principles that will help most of us make this connection.

⤳

IN TRACING MY OWN PERSONAL history, it was apparent that my early self-designed Outward Bound adventures gave way to a need to go inward, which led to an inner practice. This matured into a different style of wilderness experience that was more life-sustaining, healing, and fulfilling to that phase of my life. In wanting to share this with others, I began to facilitate inward bound healing journeys to Peru and Southern Africa. Those that join us are looking for this unique experience. They may not have scaled high mountain peaks, but they have encountered other challenges and overcome them so that self-mastery, self-concept, and self-esteem usually are not an issue.

The wild outdoors is a great teacher of self-awareness, which is the first step in connecting with the higher self. If one is not self-aware, there can be no moving toward the true self. Ego is another obstacle on the trail to the true self, and it is best for the ego to be fully developed before it can be appreciated and released. Healing occurs when we come into closer contact with the bigger picture of the true self while putting the little picture of the ego in the background. Our egos already are powerfully developed and need to be scaled down. The wilderness journey discussed here, therefore, is an internal one, and the external is de-emphasized as being food for the ego and likely to provoke a relapse back into the false nature of materialism.

It seemed that for me there had been a natural sequence of maturation, which can be summarized as follows.

My early experiences in the African bush had led to a certain level of self-concept, self-esteem, self-sufficiency, and self-mastery. This was complemented simultaneously by my medical and surgical training. In other words, my ego base was solid and reasonably secure. As described later, one could say I had focused on and developed my lower three chakras or energy centers.

When I arrived in California, many of these aspects were reinforced during my urology training, but on the other hand new circumstances occurred that highlighted the fact that my inner life was sadly deficient. For those in the medical profession in the United States today these factors can be lumped together in a phrase I have labeled "The dreaded M's": marital disharmony; managed care; malpractice; the problems confronting Medicare, Medicaid, MediCal; and, for most physicians, a sizable mortgage payment. These "M's" have resulted in a considerable amount of distress among doctors about their calling in life. The advantage of these "M's" for me, however, was that the pain induced by insecurity and frustration led to new insights and awareness that were assisted by my readings on Eastern and other philosophies.

There is a story about two Buddhist monks who were always arguing and debating with each other. One day one of the monks stood in the threshold of a doorway with one foot in the threshold and the other foot outside. He asked his friend, "Tell me, where am I heading, in or out?" His friend answered, "That depends entirely on your intention!"

⌇

MY INTENTION SHIFTED VERY DEFINITELY as a result of these factors in a distinctly inward direction. My focus became oriented away from ego and persona in favor of the higher self using yoga, meditation, and nature to assist me. This in turn allowed me to develop a model for facilitating the power of wilderness both for myself and the groups I planned to take out in the wild.

In summary:

> Outwardly directed hard skills in wilderness invoke directed
> attention and use of the left brain that lead to an increase in:
>
> - Self-concept.
> - Self-esteem.
> - Self-sufficiency.
> - Self-mastery.
>
> These hard skills and externally oriented wilderness experi-
> ences are focused around the ego (and the three lower energy
> centers or chakras of the body—see chapter nine.) However,
> once the ego is secure:
>
> - Correct intention and receptivity create self-awareness.
>
> - Intention and receptivity change as a result of life's trau-
>   mas or one's patterns of behavior being ineffective in
>   terms of inner peace.
>
> - Self-awareness results in the need for inner growth and
>   acknowledgment of the limitations of ego in our quest for
>   self-realization and transformation.
>
> - Wilderness rapture or the wilderness effect is one of the
>   many inner paths for attaining this through the medium
>   of soft skills, soft fascinations, non-directed attention, and
>   the right brain. This requires an understanding of some
>   psychology as well as knowledge of the higher energy cen-
>   ters of the body described in ancient mystical texts.

I decided to use this model in my future expression as a wilderness
healer. The information available in contemporary psychology was deficient, because in trying to be objective and scientific about a subject that
was primarily spiritual, it was not up to the task. For this I would have to
turn to ancient traditions, such as yoga, for more complete understanding.
The Eastern traditions have a sophisticated understanding of the limitations of ego and other factors for those on a path of self-transformation.
The hunter-gatherer model augmented this understanding as did glimpses
into complex systems such as Kabbalah. It was clear that there was a core

belief that permeated this mass of information with universal spiritual principles that could be applied to any inner journey and especially to the healing inner journey into the wild outdoors. The distillation and application of these esoteric principles is discussed in greater detail in chapters nine through twelve, and a summary of relevant psychology information in chapters five through eight.

CHAPTER FIVE

HEALING

WITH THE

WILDERNESS

EFFECT

- Participants were more patient, but also more irritable.

- There was an increased ability to concentrate, but more distractibility.

- Many felt good, but also terrible about the world.

- There was a feeling of inner peace, but also alienation.

- One could be more tranquil, but also more harried.

- Although less fearful of danger, some were more on guard.

- There was an ability to find joy in simplicity, but also appreciate luxury.

Overall a sense of wholeness, exhilaration, and renewal or restoration seemed to occur. Often this led to a new perspective of themselves by the participants. There was no need to be fearful because they had coped with the fear of the wild, and for adolescents this was frequently a form of initiation or a right of passage.

Most other researchers stress mediation, competence building, environmental diversity, enjoyment of nature, physical fitness, release of stress and tension, escape from noise and crowds, and outdoor learning. Kaplan is quick to point out that contemplation, meditation, and the spiritual side of nature receive the lowest priority. We can reverse this conditioning by allowing trailists the space to go inward, because given the opportunity most participants find this highly meaningful.

⤳

ROBERT GREENWAY HAS BEEN CONDUCTING wilderness trips for many years and has his own unique approach. Greenway is a master of the inner journey and uses specific techniques, such as meditation, breathing, yoga, and ritual—before and during his trips—to decrease cultural programming and to increase awareness. There is a three- to eight-week preparation period prior to entering wilderness. These practices are also important to help re-integration and ease the re-entry depression.

Before leaving for the wilderness, a group of strangers develops into a close, cooperative community. All participants are required to be fit and the groups are limited to a maximum of sixteen. Ritual is used extensively from the time the trip begins until the end. Everything except life-threatening situations is handled by consensus, empowering the group and defusing stress. There also is a solo for three to four days, singing, all-night chanting rituals, and climbs to peaks at sunrise or sunset or in silence in the moonlight. The men and women may be separated for several days and the Native American-styled sweat lodge also comes into play. Minimum-impact techniques are essential.

Greenway has observed certain patterns among the trekkers.

1. An increased sense of aliveness, awakeness, well-being, and energy.

2. A break with addictions ranging from significant to minor.

3. An increased sense of empowerment.

4. A re-entry that was initially pleasant and enjoyable, but within forty-eight hours turned to depression.

5. A major life change upon return, either in personal relationships, employment, housing, lifestyle, or academic progress.

6. Success in conquering fear and expanding limits.

7. Adoption of at least one ritual, varying from tuning into nature's cycles to chanting, yoga, and praying before meals.

8. Acknowledgment of alone time being the single most important aspect of the trip. Getting up before dawn, climbing a ridge or peak in order to greet the sun was cited as the second most vital experience.

9. Most called the trip one of the most significant events of their lives.

Greenway also discusses fear and says that it was rare not to have someone mention the subject at some point. Fear appeared to be an important issue, in spite of the fact that no hard skills, such as rock climbing and rap-pelling, were used, .

He also noted a shift in dream patterns and that most of the partici-pants noted dramatic changes in the quantity, vividness, and content of their dreams within the first forty-eight hours. Most of these changed from busy urban scenes to those of the group or some aspect of wilderness.

There was a distinct difference in the effects the wilderness had on males and females. The transition into wilderness was easier for women, the return easier for men. Women tended not to be interested in going anywhere once in wilderness, whereas men liked to explore. Women were more tuned into cycles, such as those of the moon, whereas men became more involved with meditating and chanting.

Some of Greenway's recommendations include:

- Using ritual, contemplation, and other techniques.

- Eliminating time restraints.

- Creating a community.

- Recognizing the four elements and the four directions.

- Balancing solitude and group activity.

- Practicing full honesty.

- Protecting the wilderness.

- Being sensitive about the return.

- Continuing one's inward practice after the trip.

There are many qualities in this description that simulate the San hunter-gatherer type of existence, such as egalitarianism, ritual, singing, separation of men and woman when appropriate, and connecting with the four elements and celestial events. There is little that separates participants from the effects of nature. It is this approach that is likely to put the trailist on an inward trek, and at the same time maximize restoration and healing.

RANDALL PITSTICK AND JOHN HENDEE have described a model for the use of wilderness for personal growth and inspiration. They discuss the following aspects.

1. Receptivity is necessary for personal growth to take place. Those who are complacent or in denial are less receptive and not as likely to experience personal transformation. However, those in transition and suffering emotional trauma or personal crisis—such as divorce, death of a loved one, loss of a job, and illness—are more likely to be open to what wilderness has to offer.

Greenway disagrees with Hendee's premise and says that it is often the least receptive candidate who has the greatest transformation, and vice versa. Hendee points out that it is probably this variable of receptivity that accounts for such a difference in the results of many wilderness studies.

2. Optimum Stress. Personal growth depends on the right degree of stress in wilderness, and the threshold for this depends on the individual. Stress can uncover core patterns of behavior that can then be modified for the better, although an excess of stress can be harmful and inhibit personal growth.

Greenway believes that stress stands in the way of growth and transformation and that the usefulness of stress to arouse learning is limited.

3. Cultural change and a break from prevailing norms. Wilderness offers escape from conditioning that influences so much of our behavior. Slowing down and focusing on essentials can free us from daily patterns, opening horizons to new awareness.

4. Opportunity for attunement with nature and oneself. Soft skills, such as group process, reflection, and solitude, are crucial here and can create a shift from a left-brain, to a right-brain type of activity.

5. Experiencing wilderness metaphors. This idea is similar to Outward Bound's use of metaphors, providing a new method of seeing reality from a re-framing of the old way. This may encourage leadership, creativity, better reasoning, and problem solving. Success in dealing with challenges in nature can create successful coping behavior, which then can be transferred to situations in daily life outside of wilderness.

Hendee and Pitstick state that when certain conditions are met in the wilderness, personal growth occurs in a definite sequence. These are assisted by the effect of primal influences, which lead to a sense of awe and humility in nature.

Hendee says that wilderness causes increased self-awareness, which stimulates personal growth. When old patterns of social interaction do not work, we re-evaluate old ideas and develop more effective interaction. In a milieu of honesty and trust, we see ourselves differently and change our undesirable qualities. However, if the ego defense is high and receptivity low, old patterns are replicated and no growth occurs.

⤳

MICHAEL BROWN HAS ELABORATED ON the neurophysiological implications of so-called right- and left-brain activities. It is a combination of both the right- and left-brain activities that leads to whole brain function in wilderness. This is relevant to the wilderness effect and, as we will see later, has strong correlations with yoga, Kundalini, Kabbalah, and certain shamanic techniques.

Brown emphasizes the point that most wilderness leaders concentrate on left-brain, masculine, or hard-skill activities such as rock climbing, kayaking, and skiing. It is, however, in the space of the right-brain or feminine experience that the transcendent aspect of wilderness occurs. If we are to realize the more spiritual effects of wilderness, we must use more ways to stimulate right-brain activity.

Brown also elaborates that whereas the left brain is outer-directed, purposeful, rational, and analytical and involves will, strength, and endurance as well as goal-oriented behavior and hard skills, the right brain is more inner-directed: meaningful, receptive, intuitive, and symbolic. It involves compassion, empathy, love, and the soft skills contained in such activities as contemplation, meditation, dream work, dancing, singing, art, body movement, and breath work. Other facilitators of right-brain function include relaxation, reflection, writing, poetry, visualization, art, music, dance, mime, tai chi, yoga, solitude, ceremony, the sweat lodge, rituals, rites of passage, vision questing, fasting, drumming, chanting, pain, prayer, and the use of wilderness itself. These must become part of the group interaction if we are to access our inner passage in the wild.

⤿

THE FOLLOWING IS A SUMMARY of some of the transformations that can occur as a result of the wilderness effect or wilderness rapture.

1. Empowerment; self-mastery; self-sufficiency; increased self-concept and self-esteem; self-awareness; being "more like myself;" self-actualization; and self-realization.

2. Peak experiences; feelings of awe, oneness, and wonder; transcendence.

3. A sense of humility.

4. A realization that human control over nature is an illusion.

5. Connectedness with nature and a sense of comfort in nature.

6. Increased consideration of others; more openness and affability.

7. Appreciation of simplicity and the ability to live in the present moment.

8. Renewal; increased aliveness and awakening; feeling less cluttered, more mindful and focused.

9. Release from addictions.

10. Alone, or solo time, appreciated as the most valued.

The outward journey encourages self-esteem, self-concept, self-sufficiency, and self-mastery. The inward journey opens us to self-awareness and connects us to our higher selves. The effects of this inner healing can be profound and sometimes induce peak experiences. This begs the question as to what exactly is a "peak experience"? We will see in chapter nine that this phenomenon occurs when we ascend an energy hierarchy and come into direct contact with our inner being. The potential of this mechanism in bringing us inner peace gives us cause to understand this dynamic, so that we can renew ourselves inside and outside of nature as often as possible.

❧

FURTHER READING

Greenway, Robert. *On Crossing and Not Crossing the Wilderness Boundary.* Fifth World Wilderness Conference, 1993, Norway. Vance Martin and Nicholas Tyler, eds. Golden, Colorado: North American Press, 1995.

Hendee, John C. *The Highest Use of Wilderness.* The International Wilderness Leadership Foundation Inc., Fourth World Wilderness Congress, 1987, Colorado. Deaver and Estes Park, eds. Atlanta: U.S. Department of the Interior, National Park Services, Science Publications and Office, 1987.

Hendee, John C. and Randall Pitstick. *The Use of Wilderness for Personal Growth and Inspiration.* Fifth World Wilderness Conference, 1993, Norway. Vance Martin and Nicholas Tyler, eds. Golden, Colorado: North American Press, 1995.

Kaplan, Rachel and Stephen Kaplan. *The Experience of Nature: A Psychological Perspective*. New York: Cambridge University Press, 1989.

U.S. Department of Agriculture Forest Service. *The Use of Wilderness for Personal Growth, Therapy, and Education*. Fort Collins, Colorado: Rocky Mountain Forest and Range Experiment Station, 1990.

CHAPTER SIX

FEAR

AND

STRESS

It must be a poor life that achieves freedom from fear.

Aldo Leopold

MOST PEOPLE FEAR THE UNKNOWN, but in fact it is really the known we should fear. Information that has been imposed upon us by past conditioning limits our perspective and holds us in a box of captivity. By going beyond the known—which should be feared—to the unknown—which should be embraced—personal growth is facilitated. It is, however, in this transition from known to unknown where fear and stress occur.

Fear stimulates the autonomic nervous system leading to the classical "fight or flight" reaction that also can involve freezing and feigning death. This cognitive appraisal of a "threat" varies from individual to individual and depends on each person's appreciation of the event. The evaluation may be appropriate, as when being charged by a lion, or misconceived. In spite of the recognition of danger being incorrect, the autonomic nervous system elicits its usual response. The adrenal gland releases adrenaline, resulting in all the typical symptoms, including dry mouth, dilated pupils, and racing pulse.

If we are subjected to unlimited stress, chronic elevation of adrenaline and cortisone levels can cause a spectrum of different diseases. This kind of stress, which causes distress or dis-ease, can be labeled true stress, as opposed to eustress, which can be a beneficial form of stress leading to a sense of fulfillment once resolution has occurred. One person's stress may be another person's eustress, eliciting no adrenal response.

According to yoga scriptures, the first or root chakra situated at the coccyx is an energy wheel responsible for our survival response and fight or flight reaction. Yoga philosophy teaches us that mastery of this primitive chakra is crucial before energy can be channeled upward into the higher chakras.

When nature leads to an appropriate flight or fight response, we hopefully respond correctly, and if we live to tell the tale, there is often a sense of healing. This is different from the chronic low-grade state of emergency that modern-day society creates in our autonomic nervous system. A completed first chakra response leads to wholeness and healing. Chronic stimulation of the sympathetic nervous system leads to an excess of adrenaline and cortisone, which creates high blood pressure, raises cholesterol levels, and increases atherosclerosis or hardening of the arteries. It may induce diabetes and decrease resistance to diseases particularly cancer.

Part of Outward Bound and similar organizations' responsibilities is to show control of this cognitive appraisal of fear in such a way as to extend one's boundaries and abilities without the limitations of past conditioning. Success in this regard leads to the recognition of the restrictions we place on ourselves. Fear as a result of past conditioning relies on memory, and the use of successful strategies, such as those practiced by Outward Bound, can lead to a reframing of the old programs that bind and limit us. It is in this context that overcoming fear and stress is so important in wilderness. It leads to a greater sense of the ego-self, and with the right awareness eventually to higher states of consciousness.

The causes of fear have been labeled in various ways: superstitious and religious, loss to life or limb, deep dark and steep, the unknown. The most critical of all fears, however, are ego-based. In different studies done in wilderness situations and other areas of stress, the social fears are the most prevalent, such as fear of holding the group back or making a fool of oneself. In this may lie the power of the solo journey into wilderness. When the individual is involved in a solo there is no one except nature to judge. Nature is neutral and also has its own way of humbling the ego and diminishing its significance. If we are on our own there is no reason to protect a fragile ego, and we are more able to slip out of our persona and connect with our higher self.

The greater the perceived risk, the greater the potential for personal growth and the more lasting the effects of the experience. In other words, especially when it comes to self-mastery, no pain no gain! It is also true, however, that one can have a wilderness peak experience or profound transcendent experience in nature without stress or fear being involved.

However, the hard skills type of adventure into wilderness is often connected with fear and stress, which may or may not break through into a connection with the higher self or a peak experience. More likely than not, it will bolster the ego leading to an increase in self-concept, self-esteem, self-mastery, and even self-awareness, but not necessarily an intimate connection with the true self of our inner being.

In the groups I guide into Peru and Southern Africa, participants do not have to be concerned about left-brain, hard skills in order to be comfortable; they can tap into their right-brain activity and connect with the higher self. The trips in Peru are done with the help of horses or porters to carry gear, and horses are available for those who prefer not to walk. Whether one is going to make it over the next pass is never an issue, and great pains are taken to ensure all the participants can just "be" in the wilderness without having to worry about fending for themselves. At the end of a long day, the staff erects tents and prepares food and hot drinks. On the Inward Bound trek the leader takes responsibility for the hard skills aspect of the trip and frees the group's energy for a more life-sustaining experience.

It has been said that those with the furthest to go will gain the most, and herein lies the essence of what is called "perceived risk." What feels like a life-or-death situation to one person may be a walk in the park to another. The former is far more likely to experience an impact because of the event than the latter. It also has been said that one can overload on fear and stress, and that too much can debilitate performance.

My experience in wilderness has been that "what doesn't kill you makes you stronger," even if in the moment of the experience one is not able to see the value of a severe test. The more devastating the experience, the longer it takes to integrate. Something profound is happening at a deep unconscious level, something that may never be fully appreciated. Nevertheless, sometime later there will be a sense of completion and knowing that this was indeed a valuable, though painful, event. Although the individual may be miserable and acting out in socially unacceptable ways, something else may be going on in the psyche of which others cannot be aware.

In discussing these types of occurrences with other outdoor leaders, it is usually the least likely candidate who writes years later telling of a transformational experience that the facilitator may remember as being an ordeal to the rest of the group. Often the candidate who seemed to be having the worst possible time and was being the most disruptive and irritating will come forward at a later date with what was, in retrospect, one of the most profound moments of his or her life, even if this was to the detriment of everybody else.

Stress, fear, and pain carry great power, and more primitive cultures have understood this in evolving their rites of passage or initiation ceremonies. This first chakra, fight or flight experience is essential for personal growth, and if it is bypassed there may be a deficiency that the individual may recognize as a gap in the spectrum of self-mastery. Therefore there are two, conflicting things going on: the self-mastery that occurs in the context of the hard skills of the left brain, and the more transcendent experience of connecting with the higher self at another level in the realm of soft skills in the right brain. Severe trials and tribulations also can be encountered in a feminine, soft way and overcome by the psyche at a deeper level, rather than at the level of ego to which we are so accustomed. The challenge resolved by hard skills that bolsters ego and self-esteem is always the easier one to talk about over a few beers around a campfire. The other, dealt with at a deep level in the psyche, is not something we can put on the mantelpiece and boast about, but nevertheless it may have a more profound significance. The story of Aguaman is a case in point.

⤳

A FEW YEARS AGO MY ex-wife Carol and I took a group to Peru on a transformational journey. The group separated into two after several days. I and the more physical members decided to hike the four-day Inca trail, a walk that begins at Kilometer 88, a railway stop on the way to Machu Picchu from Cusco. The trek then travels over the Andes, down into high jungle, and into the magnificent Inca ruin of Machu Picchu. The rest of the group went with Carol to the sacred valley of the Incas and then onto Machu Picchu by train and were to meet us at the hostel close to Winay Wayna on the last leg of the trail. We would be coming off the trail, whereas the other group would be walking back from Machu Picchu to the youth hostel. They would sleep the night there and wait for us to arrive the next morning.

The trailists were a group of five, including myself. In addition, we had a guide, a cook, and several porters to help carry our gear. Mike had decided to come only at the last moment; because of knee trouble he was worried about his ability to complete the trail, which goes up to an altitude of 14,000 feet. The night before we left he made his final decision to join us, and he seemed to have the necessary equipment. Ann, the one female in the group, had serious reservations about going and spent a sleepless night wondering whether she could make it into Machu Picchu on her own steam. She was in excellent physical condition and, with some encouragement, was persuaded to come. Terry (my older son), Charles, and myself made up the rest of the group of Westerners.

We took the train that leads from Cusco at 11,000 feet and got off at Kilometer 88 on the banks of the Urubamba River, which was about 8,000 feet in elevation. We crossed the river in brilliant sunshine and commenced our trek. Our plan was to do the worst part of the hike, which was almost all uphill to the camp sight at Llulluchapampa, on the first day. The next day we would go over the highest point of the trail at Huarmihuanusqa at 13,776 feet. The second night we would camp at Runqurucay and the final night at Phuyupatamarca. The last day we would climb down and meet with the rest of the group at the youth hostel. We would all visit another Inca ruin, Winay Wayna, together and—finally—walk into Machu Picchu through the Inti Puncu, the Gateway of the Sun. The trek was about thirty miles in length.

We were all in reasonable condition, and on the first day we made good time up toward our first stop. However, as we got closer to our destination the weather changed dramatically. Clouds came over and as we came into camp it began to rain. Fortunately, the Quechua porters had already erected the tents and started hot drinks and food cooking. It was to be a mystical experience in more ways than one, because we saw little of the scenery after that due to mist, clouds, and incessant rain.

The climb up to Dead Woman's Pass at 13,776 feet was pleasant enough in the cool, wet weather. As we crossed the pass and descended over the other side, the weather looked bleak. We reached the bottom of the valley, crossed the river, and ascended up the other side to Runqurucay. Here we were to spend our second night.

The path up to this magnificent ruin was steep, and turned into a river of water as we climbed it. We got into camp again with everything ready for us and the tents erected. Most of us were fairly wet in spite of our reasonably good rain gear.

By the next morning it was apparent that Mike was miserable. His tent had leaked and his down sleeping bag was soaking wet, affording him little warmth during the night. None of us was particularly dry when we put on our clothes in the morning, but we four had all had a reasonable night's sleep in dryish sleeping bags. Our synthetic-filled bags had kept us warm, even if a bit wet; down was a different story. None of the tents were waterproof, but they were adequate enough.

Mike was drenched, and we continued to walk the whole of the next day in the rain, clouds, and mist. While he walked we could hear a squelching sound as his boots created pressure against his soggy socks resulting in the affectionate title, "Aguaman." At Sayacmarca, another magnificent ruin, the weather lifted briefly, and for a few hours we enjoyed the ruins in relative dryness with an occasional hint of the sun coming through the clouds.

We continued on the Inca highway, which now took us into the *seja de silva*, "the eyebrow of the jungle." This was high jungle with orchards, bromeliads, parrots, and lush tropical vegetation that we were able to appreciate because it was close at hand and views of it were not weather dependent. As we continued on our way to Phuyupatamarca, the rain began to come down in torrents. By the time we reached this breathtaking Inca ruin, which means "Town on the clouds," the beginnings of a small mutiny had arisen. Mike was disgusted with the whole scenario and felt we were all masochists.

He could not understand why we were actually enjoying ourselves. Somehow the rest of us managed to melt into the mystical event and allow the rain and the wet to become part of ourselves. The porters, like Mike, were thoroughly disenchanted and hard put to see this as a transformational journey. They wanted to get down the thousand steps from "Town on the clouds," which was more like "Town in the rain clouds," to the youth hostel as quickly as possible where they could be dry. It seemed futile to put up our low budget tents in this rain, because we were likely to spend a cold, wet night. Our guide, Santiago, who also wanted to head to the youth hostel, had decided to stay back with a couple of the porters when he realized the rest of us had no intention of cutting the trip short. He suggested we sleep the night in a cave on the other side of Phuyupatamarca that could accommodate our now quite small group.

Mike went down with the rest of the porters and a lot of the gear at full speed to spend the night at the youth hostel. The rest of us descended the thousand steps and found the cave on the other side. We made up an intimate group, Santiago, two porters, Ann, Terry, Charles, and myself. We felt badly for Mike and were sure he had experienced the worst trip of his life. We at least had been able to get out of the wet and into a warm, partly dry, sleeping bag at night. Mike had been wet and cold, both day and night. Obviously he had been extremely angry with us, and I know he held me responsible for much of his discomfort. Although this was supposed to be the dry season—and clearly we would never have chosen rain—there was no question in our minds that the rain had succeeded in making us go inward and had put us in a completely different psychological space. The quality of the trail had been fully altered because of the weather.

We sat at the mouth of the cave together and Ann taught us a Dutch song. The rain clouds lifted, the sun came out, and we were greeted with an incredible spectacle in front of us through the mouth of the cave. The Andes were covered with snow and the sun was shining on the peaks. We saw this scene through a foreground of lush, dripping jungle vegetation. Because of the preceding two days of rain, the sight was all the more spectacular, and we were aware of a change in mood from being inward to going outward, with a new awareness of the event. We again thought of Mike who, after all his trials and tribulations, had missed this.

The next morning, after eating breakfast, we packed up and left down the trail to the hostel where we met the rest of the group and a somewhat introverted Mike.

There seemed a significant mismatch of energies, possibly because they had not been in wilderness as we had. This typified the phenomenon of re-entry depression, as there was a sense of loss as we came off the trail into the youth hostel. In spite of the fact that the rest of the group had been meditating intensely the previous few days, their inward journey was different from ours. Again, a testament to not only the wilderness, but the effect of the weather on our psychological frame of mind.

The difference in mood led to some disagreement later when we got to Machu Picchu and one of the women felt it brought out machismo in our small group. Another of the non-trail women put it differently, saying we were "empowered" by it. Whatever the effect, it was not gender related because Ann experienced it also, and none of the rest of the trailists were particularly macho in nature. My own personal bias was that of the two experiences, wilderness has greater power to turn one inward than even meditation in Peruvian power spots. The experience had been a profound example of wilderness rapture.

We took appropriate pictures, gave all the clothes we no longer needed to the porters, and paid them so they could head back to their homes. The group now walked off together to Winay Wayna. There was a clear distinction between trailists and non-trailists. Those of us returning from wilderness wanted to be off on our own for privacy and space. We were sensitive to contact with the others, wanting to hold onto the specialness that had transpired on our journey. We had been a harmonious group when we split before the Inca trail and by the time we walked into Machu Picchu, the clash of energies was starting to wear off. It was not long before we again shared a similar psychological state, enjoying Machu Picchu together.

Some time later I met Mike. Up until that point I had felt guilty because he may not have had the best experience in Peru. Mike, however, came to me and said that the Inca trail was probably the most powerful experience of his life. Something had shifted in his consciousness during that experience, but had needed time to integrate.

Someone's fearful reactions to an unfavorable event can be misleading, because what may seem to be a catastrophe at that time may prove to be transformational further down the road. These happenings speak to our subconscious, and because the mechanisms of the psyche are so complex, the effects of the experiences are equally difficult to comprehend.

CHAPTER SEVEN

WILDERNESS:

TRULY

SOMETHING

SPECIAL

❧

What wilderness does is present us with a blueprint, as it were, of what creation was about in the beginning, when all the plants and trees and animals were magnetic, fresh from the hands of whatever created them....

Laurens Van der Post

IS WILDERNESS A SPECIAL PLACE or just an ordinary part of the world where we can play out our needs for walking and hiking, river running, and various forms of adventure activity? Some wilderness researchers fail to acknowledge the special energy of wilderness and feel the need to prove scientifically that wilderness is, or is not, unique. More often than not, this takes the form of studies trying to demonstrate that the wilderness environment is particularly restorative. Naturally this begs the question as to whether there is a specific spiritual dimension to wilderness that is more powerful than anything we might encounter in a church, synagogue, mosque, or temple. Does wilderness indeed have some special quality?

Ulrich, an architect interested in these matters, proved that viewers of natural scenes have more relaxed electroencephalograms (recordings of brain-wave activity) than those watching an urban display. He noted that if individuals were shown scenes of a motor-vehicle accident, they experienced a quicker return to normal blood pressure and muscle tension if afterward they viewed natural scenes rather than urban ones.

There also is evidence to show that patients who have had major surgery and have views of trees from their rooms recover faster and need less pain medicine than those with a view of a brick wall.

Prison inmates who can see trees from their cells seem to have fewer stress-related problems than those who do not. Other studies have shown that even the most hardened criminals found work on farms and gardens meaningful. This led to changes, such as a sense of accomplishment, an increase in self-esteem, and a willingness to assume responsibility.

Rachel Kaplan has reviewed the importance of nature in our daily lives and the information can be highlighted as follows. What we see from our home window is more vital than we might think for our well-being, and access to nature from the workplace decreases work stress and increases job satisfaction. The "extent" of the nature environment is important for mental health and does not relate to the size of the area. There is a preference for trees over large expanses of ground and people are more interested in the way the space is designed. There should be a sense that there is more to explore than is immediately apparent. The proximity of nature is essential, more so than the size, and has been labeled "the accessible green." If the nature spot is more than three minutes away by foot it will not be utilized because the distance seems to be more important than the need.

Those who tend gardens are rewarded with greater life satisfaction. More important than large open spaces are trees, landscaping, and the opportunity for gardening. Directed versus non-directed attention seems relevant to gardeners' fulfillment. Those who initially begin growing vegetables change to growing flowers presumably for the pure aesthetic pleasure of this "soft" fascination.

Green and blue, so called "low-arousal" colors, produce less muscle tension and more pleasurable moods, possibly due to the fact that these colors predominate in landscapes. This is why these colors are used in hospital operating rooms.

Humans need not only clean air and water, but also light, which is critical for our well-being. Seasonal Affective Depression (SAD) or "winter blues" occurs when we are sun or light deprived. Those who work in office buildings deprived of natural light and fresh air display signs of the "sick building syndrome." This has led architects to create atria and indoor courtyards with plants and even running water to counteract this effect.

Whenever people are given a choice, they move to open land with trees on high points overlooking water. This may be an imprint in our DNA from the time we were hunter-gatherers and needed to see clearly for safety.

Many of us recall our most intense sensory experiences and memories from childhood as being related to nature. We prefer nature because it is alive, neutral, devoid of negative feedback, and gives us a sense of freedom.

Terry Hartig, Marlis Mang, and Gary W. Evans performed an experiment where they studied three groups. The first group consisted of wilderness backpackers, the second was a non-wilderness vacation group, and the third was a control group. All three were noted to be identical on initial testing, after which the first two groups took a trip. After the vacation, the researchers affirmed that the wilderness backpacking group showed better scores on not only a proofreading test but also on the so called "Overall Happiness Scale." This improvement in happiness and performance could be measured in spite of the re-entry depression that occurred in the wilderness backpacking group. Re-entry depression aside, there was nevertheless a proactive restorative effect enabling better coping with stress three weeks later.

If there is such a thing as a compassion index, I find as a physician that it is restored and maximized on return from an extended trek in nature. After that, it gradually dwindles, and after three months of intense work, the saddest of medical situations does not seem to evoke the empathetic response that it should. There is no question that wilderness has profound benefits on the abilities of this healer to heal. The injunction, "Physician heal thyself!" could not be more accurate than in this predicament. After returning from a trip whole and healed, one can be the healer one is supposed to be and give sufficient energy to the task at hand. A colleague of mine put it another way by referring to it as his SOB (son of a bitch) index. He said that if he had been working too hard or too long, an increasing number of his patients would become SOBs. When this happened he knew it was time for him to get away and replenish his burned-out psyche. He had enough insight to know that the problem lay in his perception rather than with the patient.

Hartig, Mang, and Evans were able to show, using similar parameters such as the Zukkerman Index for Personal Reactions, the Overall Happiness Scale, and a proofreading study, that even a brief nature walk provided more of a restorative effect than an urban walk or a relaxation exercise. There is evidence that there is more restoration in wilderness and nature settings. There are no studies to show that one must be immersed in it, but spending one week in a hotel in pristine wilderness is not the same as getting into wilderness as a backpacker, canoeist, or horse trekker.

This may have accounted for the significant difference in effect between our small group of Inca trailists and the non-wilderness meditation group walking back from Machu Picchu (see chapter six). On several trails I have taken that ended at the breathtaking ruins of Machu Picchu, more than half of the group would share this sense of loss coming off the trail and a desire to be back in pure wilderness. No doubt the return to hotel, restaurant, tourists, and buses had much to do with this and it might have been different if we had been Inca high priests or shamans 300 years ago, entering into this shrine for higher purposes than tourism. The extraordinary thing about the Incas or whoever it was who built these ruins is that they blend in so well with nature and do not stand in defiance of it, as do so many of the great structures built by the Greeks and Romans. Hence, to them, entering Machu Picchu would have required only a subtle shift of awareness.

In separating ourselves from wilderness with creature comforts, we do not experience the full potential of the restoration. We must become a part of the wilderness for it to bestow its benefits, which is most evident in the wholeness witnessed among the hunter-gatherers of the world. Our body must become part of the encounter and we must serve as more than just observers. One has to feel, touch, smell, and taste as well as see and hear it. There are no studies that speak to this phenomenon, and I am not aware of any investigation that has analyzed a wilderness vacation in a luxury lodge and compared it to a wilderness backpacking adventure.

The following example illustrates the difference between being immersed in nature and just watching it. A squall passed through Santa Barbara; it had been raining for days and the surf was high. My daughter Romi and I breakfasted in a restaurant on the beach and watched the waves crashing nearby on the sand. It was a special opportunity to enjoy the storm, the breakfast, and each other's company. While we ate, we watched two surfers riding the six-foot waves. As we were finishing, they came out of the surf, cold and wet, and passed by our window obviously exhilarated after their close encounter with the ocean. We could see it in their faces and eyes and hear it in their conversation. Our contact had been vicarious and enjoyable; theirs had been vital, uplifting, and inspiring.

It is likely that the more we approximate the hunter-gatherer model, the more we will discover the spiritual or self-actualizing benefit of the experience. We discover who we really are when we separate ourselves from material things that are not us. We benefit by ridding ourselves of these external encumberments that bolster our ego and prevent us from reaching the inner center of our being.

Sustaining factors that support the wilderness experience are:

- Receptivity and intent.

- Fear and stress.

- Sacred space and special environment.

- Connection with metaphors, archetypes, and signs.

- Primal, primeval, and primitive experiences.

- Humility and subordination of the ego.

- Peeling away the levels of consciousness (which leads to self-awareness, peak experiences, or moments of transcendence).

RECEPTIVITY AND INTENT

The individual searching in wilderness is likely to receive that which he or she seeks. If the idea of going into nature is to learn backpacking techniques, more than likely that will be all that is gained. If we are looking to reach a greater spiritual dimension with ourselves in the cosmos, that will probably occur.

Major figures in the history of wilderness preservation in the United States—including Henry David Thoreau, John Muir, and Aldo Leopold—chose to express themselves through the medium of wilderness and with its help become self-actualized. Visionaries such as Moses, Jesus, Buddha, Mohammed, and other sages through the ages also used wilderness for spiritual growth. The differences in receptivity and intent among participants probably accounts for the inconsistency of results found among the various wilderness studies in the literature.

FEAR AND STRESS

Manipulating fear and stress during the teaching of hard skills is most likely to lead to increased self-mastery, self-concept, and self-esteem, important first steps on the path to self-actualization. Use of soft, inner skills, however, is more likely to put one in touch with one's higher self and the transcendent, creating a more inner-directed experience, where fear and stress do not largely participate. Nevertheless, it may also be true that candidates for inner journeys into wilderness may be less far along the path to physical mastery than those indulging in hard skills. What to an Outward Bound candidate may prove no challenge at all could be a supreme physical challenge to the type of individual who finds himself or herself on a spiritual path and less accustomed to physical ordeals.

On a recent trip to Peru, the group I led was joined by a particularly interesting individual who had begun his own spiritual path many years before and had already refined his practice of meditation and yoga. He made yearly pilgrimages to India to various ashrams and would tell interesting tales of his experiences. Before we began our week's trek into the Andes up and around the sacred Apu (holy mountain) of Salkkantai, he told us about how powerful his exposure to yoga in India had been to him in a spiritual context. One would hardly have expected that wilderness on its own could in any way match what he found in India. However, this wilderness experience led to a distinct shift in his lifestyle after his return, and this must have occurred within the context of fear and stress and the profound effect of the wild on the psyche.

Once on trail it became obvious that he required a lot of energy to overcome the hardships of the journey. Rather than considering this a detriment, he used it to full effect to enter a catharsis that was particularly necessary for him at that point in time. When we got to 11,000 feet, he began to have diarrhea as well as suffer some of the symptoms of soroche, high altitude sickness. Associated with this were anxiety and some degree of disorientation that required the rest of the group to help take care of his basic needs. When it began to rain, the cold and wet created a third dimension of mild hypothermia. In spite of all these hardships, he remained uncomplaining and in good spirits. He recognized that the trials the trip was offering were a gift to process and use for personal transformation. To this individual, an experienced meditator, going inward was no new thing. It seemed what he required was an additional dimension of physical challenges offered by the wilderness.

The power of wilderness is such that it offers up to us whatever it is that we need at that point in time. Depending on our receptivity and maturity, this can be processed in such a way as to help us on our path of personal development. In the words of the Rolling Stones: "You can't always get what you want. But if you try, you just might find, you get what you need."

SACRED SPACE AND SPECIAL ENVIRONMENT

The power of one's initial experience in a novel and exotic place such as Peru is startling. These completely new and fresh exposures help us get in touch with the uniqueness of the environment by bringing us into the present moment. Some of the magic is lost on subsequent visits to the same area. Those of us who spend time in wilderness have no doubt that wilderness is more than a restorative environment and fulfills the requirements of a sacred space, possibly more so than any church, synagogue, mosque, or temple. The words of a bushveld trail guide in South Africa to his group on entering the wild say it clearly: "This is my church; don't desecrate it!" There are multi-dimensional possibilities here that do not exist in other situations. The more pristine the area the more powerful it is, hence the value of areas untrammeled by humans or, as the Wilderness Act of North America states, "Wilderness is an area where earth and its community of life are untrammeled by man; where man himself is a visitor who does not remain." The act is true to the archetype of sacred space and recognizes it as a space of numinosity where one cannot stay.

Sometimes the areas visited are so sacred they could be called power spots. When one comes into these areas, it is well to honor them, if not for their magical healing effect, then for one's own sake in the hope that the gods, spirits, or energies of the place are not disturbed.

Several years ago I took my two sons on an extended camping expedition into Botswana and the Kalahari Desert. We were joined by some family friends who also had two sons. As we were packing up the trailer to leave Johannesburg, the sons asked me if it was acceptable to pack a parasail in among our camping equipment. I declined. This was a wilderness experience and the purpose was to get away from these types of activities and connect with wilderness on a purer level.

After about a week of travel through the Kalahari Desert, having visited with my San friends, we found ourselves at the edge of Sowa Pan, which is part of the huge Makgadikgadi salt pan in the Kalahari. When we arrived at the pan it was clear to me that this place was tangibly different in the energy that pervaded earth and sky. When the parasail suddenly manifested itself out of the depths of our trailer, I could regard it only with a feeling of disgust. This was not the place to parasail, anymore than it would be appropriate in a temple. I walked off in a huff as far from the area as I could, so that I could still enjoy the serenity of the place without having to be confronted by a vision of a parasail being pulled by a whining four-wheel-drive. Nevertheless, it crossed my horizon while I was sitting on the shore watching the flamingos.

Terry, my older son, waved as he passed. Soon after, I heard a loud crash and saw my other son, Paul, driving at full speed up the shore toward me. He screamed at me that Terry had crashed into the trailer with the parasail. Paul picked me up and drove back to the scene of the accident. Terry lay on the sand next to the trailer, a metal thing with a metal cover attached to the top by strong steel hinges. The cover had been open, supported by a prop, and it was into this Terry had crashed. The driver of the Toyota had made a severe miscalculation and, while turning, had pulled him at full speed into the trailer with an impact so great that the entire top of the trailer had been torn off, metal hinges and all.

After carefully examining Terry, it was apparent that, though battered and bruised, he had not suffered any major injuries. This was a relief, especially because we were hours and miles away from the nearest hospital. We packed away the parasail, hitched the trailer to the Toyota, and made our way back down the rudimentary track. After driving for about five minutes there was a sickening thud; another unhappy event had supervened with the trailer. The entire spring on the one side had broken off, and all the trailer could do now was crab behind the Toyota in an ungainly fashion as the tire scraped along the chassis. We camped that night close to the Sowa

Pan, and the next day had to jettison the trailer at the nearest village after several strong Tswana men lifted it into the back of a Landrover and hauled it away. Terry, fortunately, was none the worse for wear even though the force of his impact had succeeded in destroying the integrity of a strong metal trailer that had survived one week of travel on the worst that the Kalahari roads had to offer.

From the minute we arrived in Sowa Pan I was aware of the geomancy that surrounded the place. An activity like parasailing seemed sacrilegious. Instead of honoring my intuition and honoring the place, I allowed the activity to proceed. In the future I will be more diligent in sacred spaces.

On another occasion I visited a friend's game farm in Zimbabwe, a few hours north of Harare, with my younger son, Paul, and younger daughter, Romi. We decided to spend the weekend hiking the farm under the guidance of a French ecologist, Hervé, who was surveying the farm for the owner, Andre. Before we left on the trek we talked about the mountain, Genya, which imposed itself on the surrounding area. Andre jokingly said, "This mountain is sacred to the Shona people and no one is allowed there without special permission." He hastened to add that we should not worry and a climb up was worth the view.

We camped that night next to a stream and a waterfall at the foot of mount Genya with the sounds of baboons barking in the rocky crags. Hervé suggested we make an early start the next morning and climb up. I mentioned to Paul and Romi that because this was a sacred place we should ask permission from the mountain spirits sometime before the morning. Both of them looked at me with amusement and a hint of disdain.

We left shortly after sunrise and started to climb. Hervé had been living in the bush for some time and had developed excellent "bush eyes." In spite of this he, followed by Paul and then Romi, literally stepped over a huge python without noticing it. It was hard for to me to appreciate how they succeeded in not seeing and not standing on the snake. Its head and neck were on the trail, the body in the thick grass. I was in the rear and called them back to look at this unique site. It was winter and the morning was cold. The snake was immobilized and could not have moved away if it wanted to. This enabled us to spend some time studying it up close, after which we continued to climb the mountain. When we reached the top and looked down to a flat ridge nearby, we noticed a large circle made out of stones. It was divided into four quadrants by more stones and looked similar to a Native North American Medicine Wheel.

When we had finished our visit and were driving back to Harare I picked up a Shona woman who was hitching a ride. When I asked about the mountain, she said, "Only the medicine men go up there, no one else is allowed." I asked, "What happens if you go up there without permission?" and she replied, "You'll see lions and snakes and things." Somehow on this occasion the opposite seemed true. I had paid my respects to the mountain spirits just before we left on the climb. Almost in minutes the python presented itself in a unique situation that gave us all, and me especially, a special connection with Genya.

There is little doubt that wilderness in general, and some areas in particular, have a certain sacredness or numinosity to them. If we are able to visit in a respectful fashion, our trip may be more meaningful and safer as well.

CONNECTION WITH METAPHORS, ARCHETYPES, AND SIGNS

If one can be propelled into a profound meditative state just by looking at a flower, how much more so when we are involved in the exquisite beauty of a completely functioning ecosystem. Metaphors, archetypes, and "signs" all seem to be more prevalent in wilderness than in any other possible situation. In terms of the Native American vision quest, these signs that arise in wilderness seem to be woven into the archetypal journey of the hero. Because of a heightened awareness or altered state of consciousness, the meaning of this sign is usually quite clear. It is only when the individual merges with nature that this sign is likely to appear, or more accurately that the sign when it does occur will be interpreted as meaningful. It is very much a part of the unconscious and will speak to us in the language of the unconscious. It does not arise cognitively out of left-brain activity, but is a function of the more symbolic and intuitive right-brain expression.

This sign, be it a metaphor, archetype, or something else, can offer a solution to one's problems and become a guide to the perplexed seeker of wisdom. The Native Americans had a sophisticated understanding of psychodynamics. In order to facilitate the process, wilderness was used as the vehicle, and fasting, solitude, pain, and sometimes hallucinogens were added to the basic medicine of wilderness. They recognized that it was usually in the outer wilderness that a sign could emerge and speak to the inner wilderness of the psyche.

Frequently the sign takes the form of an animal, which brings a message of clarity to the psyche at that moment in time. These animals have been called "power animals" by certain shamans. Don Eduardo Calderon, a Peruvian shaman, explained to a group of us visiting him that the power animal, or totem, was not necessarily a grand animal that you wanted to be, such as a puma or an eagle, but rather the animal you needed to be, such as a mouse, if this meant you needed to learn humility on your spiritual quest. He insisted that nothing happened by accident and made many references to power animals that had significant symbolic meanings. The attributes and qualities of your power animal could help you along your spiritual path.

He told us just before we left Peru after our first visit that we should be particularly cognizant of any animals we saw on our return home. After this first trip I had a considerable amount of skepticism about the meaning of shamanism and was still in the mind frame of negating and denying some of my Peruvian experiences.

Shortly after our return I walked into the family room of our house. There was a large fluttering of wings and inside the room was a large bird, not a raptor that I could easily identify, but at least as large as a red-tailed hawk. I had never seen any bird like it before. How it had gotten in I had no idea, because the windows were closed and our family room is a long way from any of the outside doors. The only available portal was the chimney. I opened the window and it flew out, but I remembered what Eduardo had said to me and a chill ran down my spine. Since that experience I have become open to the messages that animals sometimes bring me.

After being in wilderness for many days one can truly "be in the moment" in a Zen-like sense, and metaphors pop up like signs that bear profound meaning for problem-solving in one's personal life. Something complicated and insurmountable at home may become extremely simple in the wilderness environment when looked at in the context of a metaphor.

One can find solutions to any of our problems by looking at incidents in nature completely in the moment. This can lead to a profound sense of clarity and an "Aha!" response. It could be something as simple as watching a dung beetle rolling up its ball of dung in the African veld and realizing how much this might apply to one's own life's work. I clearly remember examples of powerful metaphors from nature that helped me with perplexing problems in my life.

One time I was trekking with two friends in the Umfolozi wilderness in Zululand, South Africa. My marital disharmony had culminated in a five-month separation, and I was coming to the end of a five-week furlough in southern Africa before returning to California and my life. My gut feeling was that I should end this separation and get back together with my wife and family, but I was concerned that this might not be the right decision.

Bruce, Paul, and I had been out in the bush for about five days when I woke early one morning and took a stroll to the crest of a hill to meditate. The White Umfolozi River was below me and the undulating acacia-studded hills of Zululand rolled away in different directions. The sun had just come up, and I felt it warm on my back. I was bathed with a sense of well-being and tranquillity. I closed my eyes and meditated; I do not recall for how long. There was nowhere comfortable to sit so I remained standing. My meditation seemed to be coming to an end and I slowly opened my eyes. Slightly to the left of me and only fifty yards away a small group of six Cape buffalo wended their way slowly up a hill. They crossed over and quickly disappeared over the other side.

In that brief moment I seemed fused with the group. They were in that instant a reflection of my life. There were six, which represented the six in our family. They were plodding along doing what they were supposed to be doing as an interdependent unit. Possibly like us, things were not perfect, but they belonged with and could look out for each other. Shortly after my return to Santa Barbara, the five-month separation ended. The buffalo metaphor was not contrived and did not occur out of a rationalization. It seemed to arise from a deeper level in a split second of that moment occurring in an altered state of consciousness. The clarity I derived from it told me that, at least for the foreseeable future, the integrity and health of the family resided in being together.

Native American vision quest tradition says that when one merges and becomes fused with wilderness, a sign or vision will arise that is pertinent to one's life journey. This clarity may create a "peak experience," although the sign or metaphor does not have to be spectacular. The metaphors will present themselves and the psyche will decide whether they are appropriate and where to fit them into life's context. There is some alteration in consciousness present after being in wilderness for awhile, and this is key to the experience. It is in this state that we are able to look at a scene and derive an interpretation from a deeper level. Seeing six buffalo at the Los Angeles Zoo on a Sunday visit might not lead to the same appreciation. Setting and a subtle change in consciousness bring the sign to life and carry it to a new context in that moment.

The importance of archetypes are discussed in chapter eight.

PRIMAL, PRIMEVAL, AND PRIMITIVE EXPERIENCES

Primal, primeval, and primitive experiences can help us connect with our cellular memory and the inherited intelligence of our DNA. It is only by tapping back into the primitive that we can make contact with this long forgotten part of ourselves, and wilderness is the best place to do this.

The analogy of the weaver bird fits here. One can bring a weaver bird out of the wild into captivity and away from other weaver birds weaving their intricate nests. Subsequent generations of weaver birds will continue to know how to weave nests in spite of having no contact with other birds doing so. This is an expression of instinct residing in non-learned behavior. We have similar non-learned intuitions and instincts we can tap into in the wild if given the opportunity. It is not so long ago that we were all rooted in wilderness as hunter-gatherers.

Because Africa is the cradle of humanity where we all originated, it is no coincidence that this is the most vital place to tap into such a power. We are open to these intangible benefits by connecting with the primitive force in any wilderness environment, but it is particularly available on the African continent. Our being is imprinted with long forgotten instincts, and this may be the reason that many people who travel to this vast continent feel a strong sense of connection and déjà vu.

HUMILITY AND SUBORDINATION OF THE EGO

It is especially when the ego dissolves that we can come into a greater appreciation of our true selves. For those without sophisticated esoteric techniques such as meditation, breath work, and sensory withdrawal, wilderness is an easy way. Wilderness "meditates you," whether you are aware of it or not. It makes us humble by bringing forth recognition of how insignificant we are. A feeling of having to control gives way to a feeling of letting things be. If one tries to control and conquer becoming an adversary to wilderness, nature usually will show you in no uncertain terms who is boss. Ego is the single most dangerous factor leading to disaster situations in the wild. Pride comes before the fall, which may turn out to be many thousands of feet.

The complications of high altitude sickness, such as pulmonary and cerebral edema (an excess of fluid settling in the lungs or the brain) that can be lethal, are more common in the group setting in wilderness, probably due to peer pressure and a reluctance of individuals to let the party know how they are feeling lest they hold back everyone or be perceived as not being able to "take it." Never more than in wilderness is it true to say that discretion is the better part of valor, or wisdom should supersede the ego. Paradoxically, it is the feminine approach that is safer in wilderness, and the macho attitude that can lead to disaster. Humility and subordination of ego facilitate the inward journey into the transcendent, and this journey is likely to be physically safer as well. Egomaniacal attitudes and machismo cause one to focus on goal-oriented behavior and achievement, which inhibit intuitive wisdom and can be fraught with disaster. One only need listen to some of the stories on trail as well as read some of the best-selling novels on survival situations to realize it was bad judgment and ego that got them there in the first place. Nevertheless, it is a tribute to the human spirit that, even though ego does get people into precarious situations, there are hidden forces that can help them get out again.

If we tune into nature, we may have intuitive thoughts and dreams about what is safe and what is not that keep us out of trouble in wild places. The crucial thing is to pay attention to them, because they often pop up only to be ignored.

A few years ago I fractured my wrist after slipping and falling off a high platform in the Amazon rain forest. The night before the incident I had a vivid dream of a friend I had not seen, heard from, or thought of for twenty-five years. He appeared in the dream and then disappeared. Paco was an experienced traumatologist who had worked with me for a year during my general surgery residency in Johannesburg. He had come to learn more general surgery, but being an experienced orthopedic surgeon had taught me a tremendous amount about fractures that we corrected when on call together at night. I especially remember him for one fracture that he had an ingenious way of reducing and that we encountered frequently together. It was that same Colle's fracture I sustained just hours after he appeared to me in my dream. Had I paid more attention to his apparition I might have averted a lot of pain and suffering.

PEELING AWAY THE LAYERS OF CONSCIOUSNESS

Solitude or periods of silence within the group are uniquely powerful in wilderness. There is something special about relating one to one with our self, and the classical vision quest is always a solo event. It could be that this is the last step to subverting the ego while in wilderness. When we are on our own we can let go. In order to find our Self (higher) we must lose our self (ego), or as Christ said, "He that loses himself will find himself." It is difficult to let go completely when in the company of others, and no matter how harmonious the group, we still are bound by social interaction and by some need to protect our delicate egos.

With or without solitude in wilderness the process is very much like peeling away the layers of the proverbial onion to get to its core, with the self being at the center of the onion. It seems as though at the beginning of the trail there are all sorts of layers of garbage and toxicity surrounding the true self and it takes time to unravel these to reach the center of one's own being.

Five days seems to be a minimum in which to do this, and it is interesting that the Wilderness Leadership School in South Africa has been running five-day trails into the wilderness for many years. Douglas P. Gillett et al. in *The Journal of Environmental Education* discuss the importance of time. He says that any field trip in excess of two and one half days' duration can be significant in terms of increasing self-concept among other factors. He suggests that five days is usually enough, but that less than that may not be. If one thinks of it in the biblical context, forty days and forty nights might be so profound as to forge a connection with the true self that is sufficient for enlightenment. Solitude alone may have much do with this, and one cannot help but feel certain people of great stature come out of long periods of confinement with a clearer vision of themselves and the problems around them. Naturally one has to be quite far along the spiritual path before undertaking anything as formidable as a forty-day solo.

The analogy between the layers of an onion and the five energy sheaths described by the yogi Patanjali in ancient yoga texts is an apt one. Patanjali describes these sheaths (also called layers or bodies) as follows (going from outside inward):

1. The Food Sheath or physical body.

2. The Energy Sheath or body of breath, energy, or prana.

3. The Mind Sheath.

4. The Intellectual Sheath.

5. The Bliss Sheath, or Ananda, in the center of which is the self.

The Mind Sheath, Intellectual Sheath, and ego together also have been labeled the Subtle body. The Sheath (or Body) of Bliss or Ananda has been called the Causal body. This model is extremely useful for anyone trying to understand the dynamics of reaching that self that exists in the center of our being. Jung described this as a spiral rising upward toward a peak with the self at the crest of the peak. (As you will see in chapter ten, the symbol of the spiral is an extremely important one and spans many ancient traditions.)

Ego is referred to in yoga texts as "I-ness" and has a broader interpretation than does ego in the Western psychological sense. I-ness has no self-awareness and separates us from our true self. In the West we see the establishment of I-ness or ego as desirable, whereas Eastern philosophies and

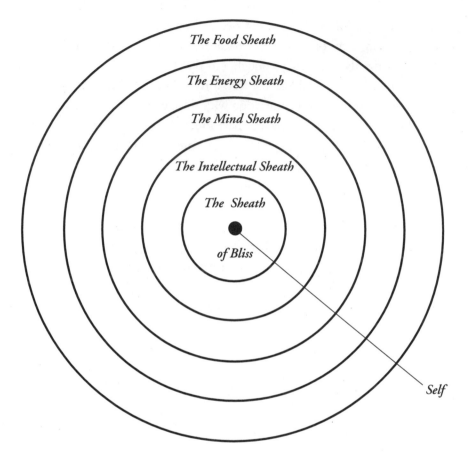

PATANJALI'S FIVE SHEATHS OF CONSCIOUSNESS.

yoga talk about spiritual evolution occurring beyond ego. Attempts to transcend ego in the West have been considered by many to be pathological.

The Mind Sheath is the primitive mind and is responsible for primitive thought, such as emotions, feelings, desires, impulses, habits, and addictions. The Intellectual Sheath, however, is the higher wisdom in us and dictates ideas, concepts, notions, beliefs, and discrimination. The Intellectual Sheath or higher mind should govern the lower mind, but does not always do so. If the Intellectual Sheath can detach from memory and sensory input and detach from ego, it can step outside of the chain of cause and effect—the cycle of Karma. If it does this there is no need to be born again.

If not, one repeats the cycle of reincarnation until we can demonstrate that the ego no longer has any binding power over our behavior. Things are done purely for their own sake and for no ulterior motive whatsoever, nor for any ego aggrandizement. A simple example of this may be charity done for its own sake versus charity done for the sake of a tax break or getting one's picture in the media. This kind of act, though superficially noble, has an ego-binding motive behind it, the consequence of which is yet another cycle of rebirth.

The Mind Sheath, or lower mind, is directly in touch with sensory input that often leads to a motor response. It is constantly in a state of flux, and without the higher mind to regulate it, has no ability to discriminate or evaluate. This can lead to anger, hate, jealousy, and other negative emotions. With the help of the Intellectual Sheath, the Mind Sheath can generate positive emotions. Without this super-imposition, the Mind Sheath resides in a state of doubt and acts on habits and impulse. The Mind Sheath can be manipulated favorably with meditation and mindfulness. For those who believe in a mantra form of meditation, it is said that the Mind Sheath activities that are often undesirable can be replaced with mantra. In Zen traditions, mind is modulated and governed with mindfulness to the extent that mindfulness should extend into all our daily activities, from the most mundane to the most sublime, making all of them a form of meditation.

Simplistically speaking, there are two enemies preventing us from reaching our higher self. The first is ego or I-ness and the second is the uncontrolled Mind Sheath. Both of these are intimately connected and governed by the Intellectual Sheath, and hence the three form a triad. The Mind Sheath believes that the primitive emotions arising from it represent truth when, in fact, this is the notorious monkey that sits on our shoulder chattering messages that lead to delusion. It is the Mind Sheath that is operating when our emotional garbage comes up in wilderness or anywhere else. For some, this garbage can be modulated and governed by the Intellectual Sheath. These people take responsibility for these emotions and realize that this garbage is not them, it just needs to be processed and released appropriately. There are others less evolved along the spiritual path in whom the emotions of the Mind Sheath become reality. This results in denial of self-responsibility and assignment of blame. Judgment is a powerful tool for the

Mind Sheath, and judgment and blame are frequent manifestations of this layer or sheath during the stress of wilderness situations.

It is possible to tap into the five sheaths of Patanjali during a wilderness trek or any other spiritual endeavor to access the higher self. The wilderness journey is one of the most powerful tools for personal transformation because it is multifaceted and taps into all components feeding the psyche— from fear, primal experiences, ego, and humility to archetypes, metaphors, and the higher self itself.

It would appear that we begin the journey with our physical body or Food Sheath and go inward from there. There are times, as the wilderness works its magic, that we tap into our Energy Sheath or body of prana so we may develop unexplained energy and ability to walk all day and carry the heaviest pack. We are tapping into a different energy supply that seems limitless and sometimes leads to extraordinary physical feats such as those done by martial artists as they connect with chi or other similar energy phenomena.

Unfortunately, the Mind Sheath is often a large part of some people's journey and they are unable to get out of the space of blame, judgment, envy, hate, and other negative emotions. These people often take longer to integrate and appreciate significant shifts in wilderness. There is no doubt that exposure to the multifaceted dynamic of the wild will confront us with the psychic debris we least want to confront. This arises from the Mind Sheath.

Others govern the Mind Sheath with the Intellectual Sheath, but may still be in the space of the mind. However, there is no acting out and the rest of the group does not suffer. They are nevertheless in a state of internal conflict where mind is bubbling up and wants to take over, but the higher wisdom says otherwise. Still others have a highly developed sense of the higher mind or Intellectual Sheath. They are in the space of higher wisdom and are more closely in contact with the next level of the Causal body, or the Sheath of Bliss. Because ego and mind are so interdependent, these trailists are not so strongly attached to defending their egos.

It is at the point that we make the leap into the Sheath of Bliss that we start to connect with the higher self. Many of us may experience this at some stage of the journey and recognize it as being a momentary profound change in our state of consciousness or as a peak experience. This often is transient and, as we try to hold onto it, it disappears. The peak experience may be the ultimate expression of wilderness rapture.

On one occasion, a group of us were horse trekking in the Peruvian Andes up and around the holy mountain, or Apu, of Salkkantay. We had crossed over the pass at 16,000 feet and were descending into the high jungle on the other side. By this time we were six days into the journey, and with the help of various techniques including meditation, breath work (Pranayama), and singing, many of the group were beginning to tap into deeper levels of being. It would be no exaggeration to say that they were having fleeting peak experiences and were connecting with the Sheath of Bliss.

Researchers in Transcendental Meditation refer to the "Superfluidity State." This is an effortless state that creative people enter into, where projects seem to progress of their own accord. Actions become automatic and just "flow," and concentration appears minimal. There is a different quality to consciousness and no doubt a slowing of the brain-wave frequency.

On this particular trek a rock fall had preceded us, probably by several weeks. The trail passed along the side of a cliff face and was partly obliterated by the fallen rocks, trees, and debris. Without so much as a thought, the riders in the front—at least half of whom had never been on a horse prior to this trail—negotiated their way across the precipice, over the avalanche, and onto the safe side of the face. Those bringing up the rear of the group who were not in this altered state of consciousness were appalled at what they saw. They could not believe that these five people had made the crossing without looking back or having a second thought.

This did not occur out of bravado, but rather out of a state akin to superfluidity. On questioning the group afterward it was apparent that they were in an extreme state of relaxation, well aware of a change in consciousness. Most of the riders in retrospect admitted that in any normal state of awareness they could not conceive of doing what they had done. The horses also had not hesitated, because the riders had not been in the least bit fearful and no "fear pheromones" were being secreted. The rider, the horse, the avalanche, and the cliff face all had merged into one effortless experience. In that brief period, which also could be called a peak experience, the trailists were connecting with the Sheath of Bliss and coming closer to the center of their being and the higher self.

CHAPTER EIGHT

ARCHETYPES

C. G. Jung describes archetypes as universal themes running through myths, fables, fairy tales, sagas, legends, and stories, each of which has characteristics common to all cultures. For example, the archetype of the tree in all traditions is the link between heaven and earth. Archetypes exist in the human unconscious and the collective unconscious and can be compared to the instinct of an animal.

There are numerous archetypes, but particularly appropriate in wilderness are the hero, the Earth Mother, the persona, the self, the shadow, and the sacred space archetype.

Our persona or mask tries to mimic our ego ideal and, like our ego, conceals our true self or true nature from us. The archetype of self is different than that described in yoga and Eastern philosophies. Jung regarded the self as the central archetype of wholeness comprising the total personality including the ego. The individual can self-realize only if the ego is willing to subordinate to the self. Eastern thought believes that *samadhi,* or ecstasy, can only be attained if ego or I-ness is completely transcended. Jung argued that samadhi was actually a loss of consciousness, and that clarity could occur only in the context of ego. Western conditioning supports the argument that ego transcendence is pathological. No election campaign would succeed if its delegate adopted a strategy of ego effacement and stressed the importance of the higher self rather than the American dream. The Dalai Lama would be unlikely to win a seat in Congress.

The archetype of sacred space is very much part of the wilderness journey. Difficult to reach, it is mystical and numinous. Humans cannot remain there, and usually the individual comes back from the sacred space with a gift or Grail or a vision of himself in his community and place in the universe. The seeker often is transformed by the experience.

The shadow archetype will be discussed in chapter eleven relating to the control of judgmental attitudes while on trail. The Earth Mother archetype is easily understood by the San concept of the creation, by Bisi, the Great Spirit (see chapter two.)

Joseph Campbell says, "The hero ventures forth from the world of common day into a region of supernatural wonder. Fabulous forces are there encountered and a decisive victory is won. The hero comes back from this mysterious adventure with the power to bestow boons on his fellow man." There is a Sanskrit chant that translates, "May the hero awaken from forgetfulness and transcend all anxiety and sorrow."

In the context of Kabbalah, the hero is seen as having to conquer the serpent, which is wound around the central trunk of the Tree of Life, in order to reach Keter, the highest sephira and the place of enlightenment (see chapter ten).

These examples are typical of the archetype phenomenon where the same theme is similar in the eyes of an American, Joseph Campbell; an Indian Sanskrit saying; and the Jewish mystical belief of Kabbalah. These archetypes are an essential part of our psyche and their importance needs to be acknowledged.

The journey of the hero, the journey of initiation, or any rite of passage has been defined by Arnold Van Gennep as occurring in three distinct phases: severance or separation, threshold or the journey itself, and incorporation or integration. The hero's journey is the quest for one's own higher self, a journey into one's own psyche. In the first phase of separation the hero hears the call to adventure. He must either follow it or kill something within. This call is a yearning for the extraordinary. The first level of resistance (for example, work, home, spouse, children, friends) must be overcome, and once this is done, guides assist the hero by pointing out the dangers and showing the way. This is the phase where synchronicity may appear. Jung described synchronicity as a meaningful coincidence where two events occur simultaneously, linking the inner psyche with the outer event. For example, one makes a decision to take a spiritual trip to Peru and a brochure arrives that day describing the very trek you wish to take. The hero may be armed or given a symbol of power, such as a sword in the classical tales of old. In the context of today, this is more likely to be some form of knowledge, say in the form of a book or a teacher to help one on the way.

In the West our rites of passage pale by comparison. A bar mitzvah approximates a formalized rite, but the worst the child can be concerned about is embarrassment because he did not say the portion of the Torah as well as he might. The same may be said for confirmation. There is no physical danger or pain, and the three phases are not part of the process or its preparation. There is no real separation from the maternal. There is a threshold phase that is intellectual, but no physical dragon need be faced, nor is there any incorporation phase. The youth's life is only just beginning in the West, and many skills will be learned before incorporation occurs back into the society. Parents can tell a pampered Western teenager how brave he is, but on the inside he knows differently. The feeling must be earned at a deeper level.

A certain amount of bravado goes on between teenagers of today that is somewhat an attempt to connect with this archetype. Part of the energy that is generated often has to do with female onlookers, or at least the peer pressure of fellow males. In the traditional initiation ceremony, no females are present and the process is ritualized into something far more meaningful. The elder, wise males of the society are in attendance, and pressure comes from a different source. The youth will carry this all his life and retrieve it from his psyche when the need for courage and fortitude arises. Armed with this past experience he can believe in his ability to handle whatever comes his way. I cannot help but think that this inner strength has enabled many Africans to endure with equanimity and courage the numerous trials and tribulations the continent continuously offers up to them.

It is in this that the power of the rite of passage resides: the feeling that one has come through an awesome ordeal and that whatever life brings one will be able to go back to that space and say, "I can cope now as I have coped before."

～

IT IS EASY TO FORMULATE any wilderness journey of sufficient duration into the three phases described by Van Gennep.

In the first phase of severance, we must separate from past conditioning and old patterns of behavior. We drop away from our personas of teacher, nurse, lawyer, engineer, and doctor so that we can reach into something fresh and new about ourselves. With an open, empty mind, not filled or restricted by stale conditioning, we are more able to receive what the sacred space of wilderness has to offer. Some wilderness researchers interested in the spiritual side of the wild even suggest changing one's name, at least for the duration of the trip.

During the threshold phase our emotional baggage will come up on the trail as a manifestation of another archetype, the shadow, where we project our dark side onto others in the form of judgment and blame. There must be a forum for expressing feelings; this takes the form of a talking or council circle, which helps to defuse touchy situations. This is not an attempt to have psychotherapy in the wilderness, but there has to be an outlet for some of the powerful emotions that arise. Participants must take responsibility for their own journey, both physical and spiritual, and in the circle are allowed to discuss only their own feelings. No finger pointing is permitted.

Time is allotted for discussing the ramifications and detrimental effects of blame and judgment. Because fear is a large component of this phase it is discussed in detail, and releasing one's fears is ritualized into one or another ceremony that seems appropriate for the group and the situation at hand.

Finally, at the end of the trail we enter the phase of incorporation or integration, where re-entry depression is sometimes a powerful factor. This must be discussed, and the coming out should be designed to be mindful.

Very often the group realizes how profound the wilderness effect has been only on the re-entry phase. Others they encounter seem profoundly different. Voices are too loud and there is a general feeling of sensory overload. This is often the first inkling to the trailist that they have in fact been in an altered state of consciousness. The inward aspects of the trip are best kept to oneself, because often they are misinterpreted by others. The more outward components are easily described and are less likely to lead to discord. The participants are discouraged from making any major life changes until these powerful effects have subsided several weeks later.

Nevertheless, the "real you" is likely to be who you were out on trail when you were connecting with your higher self. As we readapt to the various toxicities that society imposes upon us, this "you" may be supplanted by a less true or desirable version. We all need to remember who we really are, and if we cannot carry this back with us permanently into our lives, we should at least reconnect with it from time to time by making contact with our higher selves through some form of spiritual practice. The subconscious effect of the trip might continue to work for many months and manifest itself in different ways including major lifestyle changes.

Practices such as breath work, meditation, and yoga that have been introduced on the trip are encouraged afterward. Some small practice needs to be developed that can take the form of a regular hike or perhaps gardening on weekends, where one can reconnect with the inner journey. The overwhelming overload of materialism, external stimuli, and food for the ego tends to suck people back into former ways of being and old patterns. A regular connection with some form of discipline can prevent this and help us reconnect with our inner being. The importance of the Buddhist concept of a Sangha, or community, is stressed for those who are able to connect with others so they can practice together. The group energy is self-supporting and more powerful.

The hero may return with a profound vision, or more often just a sense of clarity of how to be better in the world. This may translate into doing one's existing job with more compassion and intensity, and not necessarily making dramatic changes in one's life. There is always a choice of changing what we are doing or changing the way in which we are doing it. The same is true for relationships that can either be given up or negotiated in a different way. A regular practice and group support go a long way in preventing the "fall," the giving up of the spiritual path.

Managing the re-entry or incorporation can be summarized as follows:

- Acknowledge the re-entry depression as a gift resulting from a profound encounter with the true self. It is an indicator of a prior altered state of consciousness.

- Separate needs from wants on the return. It is the want and not the need that will sabotage a successful integration. Beware the seduction of materialism. There is nothing wrong with materialism as long as the energy required to sustain it does not take us away from "following our bliss."

- Practice the walk and suppress the talk; live the vision rather than describe it. Family and friends are more likely to pay attention to a shift in behavior for ·the better than to any transformational experience described in words.

- Do not dive back into old habits and addictions. Substitute a form of spiritual practice that is enjoyable, practical, and likely to last. One cannot fight the difficulties of modern-day society without the help of some method of going inward. This does not have to be anything esoteric; surfing may be more powerful than meditation, gardening more helpful than Tai Chi.

- Develop a community that can be self-supporting. There is synergy in group activity where 2+2=5 and 5+5=15, in terms of spiritual energy.

- Live out your vision, be true to your own myth or follow your bliss (Joseph Campbell).

- The essence of incorporation is to give away the gift gained from the journey. This seemingly altruistic act has powerful consequences for the giver who benefits just as much as the receiver if not more.

↬

I don't know what your destiny will be but one thing I do know, the only ones among you who will be really happy are those who have sought and found how to serve.

Albert Schweitzer

↬

FURTHER READING

Campbell, Joseph with Bill Moyers. *The Power of Myth*. New York: Doubleday, 1988.

Foster, Steven with Meredith Little. *The Book of the Vision Quest*. New York: Prentice Hall Press, 1988.

Foster, Steven with Meredith Little. *The Roaring of the Sacred River*. New York: Prentice Hall Press, 1989.

Jung, Carl G. *Man and His Symbols*. New York: Doubleday, A Windfall Book, 1983.

Madhi, Louise Carus, Steven Foster, and Meredith Little. *Betwixt and Between: Patterns of Masculine and Feminine Initiation*. LaSalle, Illinois: Open Court, 1988.

Van Gennep, Arnold. *The Rites of Passage*. Chicago: The University of Chicago Press, 1966.

Wilmer, Harry A. (M. D.) *Practical Jung*. Wilmette, Illinois: Chirom Publications, 1988.

Zimmerman, Jack and Virginia Coyle. *The Way of Council*. Las Vegas: Bramble Books, 1996.

CHAPTER NINE

CORE BELIEFS:

KUNDALINI,

KIA,

AND THE

PEAK

EXPERIENCE

Whatever we see or don't see, whatever exists, right from the earth to the sky is nothing but Kundalini. It is the supreme energy which moves and animates all creatures, from the elephant to the tiniest ant.

Swami Muktananda

BECAUSE THIS BOOK CONCENTRATES ON the inner journey in wilderness, it is important to develop a model with which we are able to understand the dynamics of the transcendental event. Wilderness rapture occurs when we come into contact with our higher selves while in nature. Understanding this effect requires that we learn more about other methods for attaining the higher self from spiritual sages who have perfected this in the past. If we want to have a deeper connection with our true selves using nature as a vehicle, we need a map to follow the inner passage just as much as we need a topographical map to follow the outer journey.

The Kundalini energy is said to pervade the entire cosmos, be present in every particle, and operate at every level. By coming to appreciate this power, we can gain understanding not only of ourselves but also of the cosmic energy of the planet and the whole universe. If we wish to develop our awareness of the "spirit that moves in all things" in the wild, the more we know of psycho-spiritual technology the better.

Kundalini and Kia (the trance phenomenon of the San) have many similarities, and because San spirituality was born out of the wilderness it is vital to look at this in the light of the other. Kia has been poorly studied because not only are the San hidden in the depths of the Kalahari but also they had no written language and the magic has been handed on by word of mouth. It is clear, however, that Kia is another manifestation of the Kundalini energy that has healed and harmonized the San in Southern Africa for eons.

I have been questioned from time to time about the relevance of these ancient spiritual principles to the wilderness. The wilderness effect or wilderness rapture has never been clearly defined, but its properties include a feeling of inner peace, tranquillity, oneness, and wholeness. This suggests that it is a spiritual phenomenon catalyzed by the multifaceted beauty of the wild. Maslow would have called this a peak experience. A yogi or a Buddhist would call it by another name.

Just as medical students must learn and be aware of the basic functions of anatomy, physiology, pathology, and pharmacology in order to function as competent healers, we need a thinking framework in order to appreciate the transcendental journey through our inner and the outer wilderness. As medical students and later as doctors, we forget and never use much of what we have learned but that does not invalidate the knowledge itself—which can be retrieved anytime it is deemed useful to help us on the path of healing. In a similar way if we are to talk about such lofty concepts as wilderness rapture, transcendental, and peak experiences, it behooves us to appreciate the ideas of spiritual giants that have preceded us.

Also, on delving a little deeper into these ancient wisdoms, it is apparent that there is a core belief that permeates through all the teachings that we can carry with us on our own path as we trek through the sacred space of the wild outdoors and access our inner being.

Transcendental has been defined as beyond ordinary limits, beyond the bounds of human experience, connecting with the supernatural. This mystical event often promotes feelings of awe, wonder, at-oneness, harmony, and inner peace. Maslow called it the peak experience. A similar phenomenon has been described in Eastern traditions as Samadhi or Nirvana. The difference between Maslow's peak experience and these more esoteric versions seems to be one of intensity and, in the case of the yogi, the ability to induce the event at anytime and remain in that state as long as desired. The peak experience, on the other hand, is usually a very transient occurrence, and when we try to hold onto the sheer pleasure of it, it disappears. We invoke our analytical left brain to maintain the wonderment and the minute we do so it disappears. Because the inward journey in and outside of nature often leads to mystical experiences, one must consider the semantics of the process to appreciate it better.

According to Maslow, a peak experience occurs when we encounter transcendent ecstasy. *Ecstasy* is Greek for "standing outside oneself." It is a change in consciousness implying transcendence or at least partial transcendence of the ego, and is associated with bliss. It is accompanied by emotional rapture, mental exaltation, vision of another world, a great mystical event, illumination, revelation, insight, or awareness of becoming different.

Maslow found that since there was no effective way to describe the ineffable, most people never volunteered that they had these experiences unless directly questioned. We tend to forget, rationalize, or trivialize some of our most precious moments. He noted that the two easiest ways to encounter a peak experience were through classical music and sex. There were numerous other triggers, so many in fact that it became necessary to generalize rather than list them all. Natural childbirth was a potent stimulus, as was any event promoting pure joy and happiness, pure excellence, pure truth, pure goodness, and pure justice. It is likely that the people whom Maslow studied were not wilderness enthusiasts because peak experiences are common in those venturing into the wild and the power of nature to evoke this response is not stressed in his writings. In the word *pure* is the implication that the encounter occurs for its own sake and there is no ulterior ego-related motive. He says that great classics of music, dance, and rhythm, and especially drumming are powerful stimuli as are love, reverence, and awareness of the body. Maslow emphasizes the importance of pain as another stimulus for experientially empty people who need a more intense catalyst to tune into their inner being. This may be an important factor operating in the wilderness setting as well. Mathematics, science and art can have similar effects to great music. The unraveling of a scientific mystery can lead to ecstasy in the investigator when a crucial insight proves to be correct.

The psychology literature seems deficient when it comes to describing mystical events and therefore we need to look at ancient traditions for greater understanding.

In yoga, *Samadhi* means ecstasy and is the final limb of the yoga path. It is accompanied by complete sensory inhibition and sensory withdrawal with the merging of subject and object into a single experience. It has been described as that phenomenon where the knower, the known, and the process of knowing are fused into one. Yogis have quantitated it as having the intensity of "12 meditations." Samadhi occurs when one connects with the transcendental self, or Atman, and can lead to self-realization or liberation by transcending ego and thereby destroying this yoke or noose that limits our existence. The yogi in this state becomes one with the cosmos and realizes that he or she is the absolute as the psyche, or mind, merges with the higher self, or Atman. This state is accompanied by magical powers, one of which is control of heat.

> *As salt mingles with and dissolves in water, similarly the merging of the mind and the self is Samadhi.*
>
> Hatha Yoga, Pradipika

⤿

IN BUDDHISM, THE CONCEPT OF Nirvana is similar and comprises a meditative state of sensory withdrawal and ecstatic transcendence. Nirvana means extinction or emptiness and occurs when all thought and the ego personality are transcended and one becomes empty of a separate self. It is a state of complete inner stillness, "windlessness" or "non blowing" accompanied by total absence of sensory input. In this state there is cessation of desire, a condition in Buddhism equivalent to enlightenment.

> *The Nirvana is a realm where there is neither earth nor water, neither fire nor air, neither ether nor consciousness...neither this world nor any other world, neither sun nor moon.*
>
> Buddha in the Udana

⤿

IN ORDER TO UNDERSTAND TRANSCENDENCE, ecstasy, the peak experience, Samadhi, or Nirvana fully, we need to look at a psycho-spiritual model of its mechanism. It is through the yoga description of the Kundalini energy that we can best come to understand the dynamics of these mystical states, which have similar qualities. Excellent descriptions of this sophisticated technology are found in the yoga literature. This becomes even more apparent with the availability of simple English texts translated from the Sanskrit.

Usually, before we can understand something we have to put language to it so we can begin to make sense of a concept. It is said that the Native North Americans were unable to see the first ships that arrived on the east coast of the continent, because they had no concept that these existed and no words to describe them. It was easier for their consciousness to ignore the vessels that were to bring their nemesis to North America. Most of us ascribe to the doctrine of "seeing is believing," when often it is the other way around; unless you believe it first, you will not see it. A good example of this is the recent three-dimensional illusions by N. E. Thing Enterprises called *Magic Eye: A New Way of Looking at the World.* "By staring into seemingly abstract fields of color, one can come to appreciate a remarkable 3-D image with astounding depth, clarity and color."

Without knowing this was possible and without having the technological background to present it to people, one could look at this abstract all day and never know what lay beyond. The same can be true of energy centers in the body: unless one is aware this is a possibility, one is unlikely to experience the sometimes subtle manifestations that easily are discounted. Contemporary research using modern recording devices confirms that experienced meditators can project energy out of these energy centers.

These manifestations are, however, not always so subtle. When they occur in full force they can be so frightening and profound to the uninitiated that they can be misinterpreted as a form of psychosis rather than the natural flow of spiritual energy. Wilderness leaders and educators need to be aware of some of the manifestations of this powerful energy so they are more able to appreciate and deal with it in the back country. It is even more apt to occur in those who enter the wilderness sanctuary for spiritual reasons such as a vision quest, where fasting and being alone can accelerate the movement of this powerful force.

Many people in the West now are practicing Eastern techniques such as yoga, meditation, and Tai Chi, and this phenomenon is becoming more commonly recognized.

Christina and Stanislav Grof have studied the subject extensively and formed a "Spiritual Emergency Network," which is their title for a Kundalini hot line. The appreciation of this Kundalini energy was first appreciated by Grof during his research with the drug LSD. The arousal of such power can be terrifying to the neophyte, and many Westerners may not be in a position to handle the emotions that result. Psychedelics are another way of experiencing the Kundalini and may help open the door for those who have difficulty breaking away from stale conditioning. However, once the door has been opened, then the real work begins.

Drugs allow us to taste the beyond but do not make us masters of the transcendental.

Swami Satyananda

&

To fully understand wilderness rapture, some time and space will be spent on Kundalini and chakras. It is possibly the affinity with the Mother Earth and the cosmos that has enabled the San to transcend and move this energy without the use of hallucinogens. Their closeness and attunement to the Kalahari, together with clapping, dancing, and chanting, create this powerful phenomenon. The Kundalini is potential female energy, or Shakti energy, waiting to happen. Close contact with the feminine dimension of Mother Earth may be the ultimate tool for contacting the higher self, and hence for self-healing and restoration.

When discussing wilderness rapture, we must go beyond modern-day psychology to another model that is more complete, even if not completely scientific. We can believe it exists because it is possible even today to witness the Kundalini phenomenon as well as some of its remarkable attributes, such as the ability to handle fire, experience clairvoyance, and heal. Watching a San dancer handle fire and come out unscathed gives credence to the fact that something profound is happening even if we do not fully understand it. Kundalini, although a somewhat obscure subject to a conventional Westerner, is the gateway to the transcendent and therefore is vital in helping us explain our own mystical experiences in and outside wilderness.

It has been said that any mystical event that occurs is the result of some movement of energy within this system. Since this will lead to a subjective phenomenon, the manifestation of this spiritual force is likely to be different in all of us. Just because our interpretation may differ from the classical descriptions and may not sound quite as intense, we should not discount it. It needs to be validated in the light of each person's own religious and cultural context. This is where the San may have an advantage. Since they cannot read or write and their tradition is an oral one, apprentices of the Trance dance are not prejudiced by fixed, written descriptions of the past. Their only record from times gone by are the magnificent renditions of this form of spirit flight on the rock surfaces of the subcontinent.

In Sanskrit, *chakra* means a wheel; the chakras in the body are felt to represent wheels of energy. There are seven main chakras that correspond loosely to autonomic nervous plexuses or nerve stations found along the spinal axis.

Nadi in Sanskrit means a stream, and nadis are ducts or channels along which the life force travels as a current of energy. These nadis are similar to the meridians described in the Chinese acupuncture system and in Taoist literature. There are at least 72,000 nadis in the body, and some say as many as 300,000.

Of the thirteen main nadis, the three most important originate at the base of the spinal axis two fingers above the anus where the first chakra is situated. These three are the Ida, Pingala, and Sushumna. The Ida begins on the left and is the pale, cool, or moon (*Tha nadi*) representing the feminine. It also corresponds to the para-sympathetic nervous system that contracts or restrains. The Pingala on the right is the red, hot or sun (Ha nadi) that represents the masculine. It corresponds to the sympathetic nervous system that expands or facilitates. (In the Western medical sense, the parasympathetic and sympathetic components of the autonomic nervous system balance control of automatic bodily functions. The meaning of Ida and Pingala goes beyond the simple control of bodily functions.) Sushumna is the central and most critical nadi and runs up the axis of the spine. This is the pathway for the Kundalini energy. Sushumna begins at the base of the spine and travels all the way up to the crown of the head where it ends in the seventh chakra four finger breadths above the crown.

The Ida and Pingala wind around the Sushumna helicly and meet at each chakra. They end behind and between the eyebrows, at the sixth chakra, and then travel to the left and right nostril respectively. The Ida, or feminine principle, therefore is present in the left nostril, whereas the Pingala, or masculine principle, is present in the right nostril. This is the basis of sophisticated yoga breathing techniques called pranayama, which rely on balancing the energies of the masculine and the feminine, the sun and the moon, the *Ha* and the *Tha* (Hatha) by utilizing each nostril in different ways.

Usually consciousness is dominated by the sun and moon nadis, and the prana, or life force, moves up and down the Ida and Pingala, leading to externalization of attention. With the use of pranayama (breath control) as well as other austere yoga techniques, prana can be directed from the Ida and Pingala into the Sushumna or central axial channel causing stimulation of the Kundalini energy that resides there. It may be no coincidence that the Ida and Pingala spiraling around the Sushumna and meeting at these chakra points resemble the DNA helix described by Watson and Crick, and this may have tremendous relevance to vibrational changes that occur at a cellular level during different states of consciousness. The Kundalini principle is thought to pervade every atom in the cosmos and therefore must also apply to our cellular molecular structure as well.

The Kundalini is potential female energy that lies dormant in the central column at the base of the spine and is represented symbolically by an archetypal serpent.

The seven chakras can be described as follows.

1. The **first or root chakra**, resides in the perineum or at the anus and corresponds to the earth element. This is where our fight or flight reaction occurs. It is our energy center for survival. The Ida, Pingala and Sushumna originate here, as does the Kundalini serpent power.

2. The **second chakra** is situated in the genital area and corresponds to the water element. This is the center for procreation and propagation of the species and is regenerative.

3. The **third chakra** rests in the solar plexus and corresponds to the fire element. This is where ego, ambition, achievement, and vanity arise, and it is the seat of anger. It is with this chakra that we manifest our power base in the world, and this eventually determines who we become in a materialistic sense. It is with this chakra that we conquer the challenges life presents to us.

The first three chakras all are manifested in the first or Food sheath of Patanjali (see chapter seven). These three are very much part of the physical body and how it functions. They are below the diaphragm and have been called the lower chakras.

4. Ascending above the diaphragm one enters the realm of the higher chakras. The **fourth, or heart chakra**, represents the air element. This is the chakra of love, empathy, and compassion. The symbol of this chakra is the six-pointed star or hexagon, which is identical to the Seal of Solomon or Star of David seen in Kabbalah.

5. The **fifth, or throat chakra**, is the place of the ether element. This is the seat of creative expression in speech, sound, poetry, mantra, writing, art, dance, and dreams.

6. The **sixth chakra, or third eye**, is behind and between the eyes. Here lies our intuitive sense, or ability to have paranormal powers. This chakra represents the sixth sense, so important in the life of the shaman or the hunter-gatherer. It is also this chakra that may give us a "gut" feeling, which if acknowledged and acted on can keep us safe in the wild outdoors, Once one's Kundalini energy has risen this far, siddhis, or

THE CHAKRA SYSTEM.

magical powers result. These are thought to deter enlightenment if they become an end unto themselves.

7.   The **seventh chakra**, or crown chakra, is the center of enlightenment, Samadhi, or Nirvana. This is the place of the transcendent experience and is where Ananda or Bliss and Unity
consciousness occur. This is where the individual self dissolves and the observer, the observed, and the process of
observing become fused into one. Even greater magical powers occur in this space of the thousand-petaled lotus. Shiva,
the male principle, resides here.

The hunter-gatherers are in continuous and intimate relationship with four elements (earth, water, fire, air) and do not have far to go to enter the realms of the ethers, the paranormal, and the transcendent. It is possibly this affinity to the elements that gives them the facility to impel the Kundalini to ascend. We can also experience this connection and a feeling of complete harmony and inner peace after being in wilderness for extended periods. As the energy in our chakras moves upward into and beyond the heart, we may experience fleeting glimpses of this "unity consciousness" where the "I" becomes "We" and the group perceives itself as a single unit.

In psychology jargon the consecutive phases of team growth or group interaction have been described as "Forming," "Storming," "Norming," and "Performing." In the first three phases "I" predominates. It is only in the last phase of performing that "I" falls away and the "We" of the group takes precedence. This is true for the group process in wilderness as well, possibly at a more penetrating level as nature works her magic on our chakras. It would be a misstatement to say that this group phenomenon in any way resembles the ecstasy achieved when the seventh chakra is opened, but it is interesting to speculate on the mechanism of the disappearance of duality as the team process matures.

The Kundalini energy is potential female or Shakti energy and is represented symbolically by a coiled snake twined three and one-half times around the base of the central column, or Sushumna nadi. Here it remains with its tail in its mouth blocking the flow of energy in the central channel until the energy is balanced between the Ida and Pingala, or feminine and masculine nadis, which allows prana or energy to be directed into the central column. This awakens the sleeping serpent, or Shakti energy, and the Kundalini rises up the central column or Sushumna. If the serpent power is fully activated it ascends, charging and energizing each chakra as it goes.

When Shakti and Shiva meet at the thousand-petaled lotus, Samadhi occurs. The peak experience described by Maslow has similarities to this.

A good example of this form of peak experience is described beautifully by Laurens Van der Post when he returned to the South African bush after an internment by the Japanese in the World War II. As he walked down to the river, a huge Kudu bull (known for its massive, majestic, spiraling horns) stepped out of the bush in front of his path.

> *As I saw him, he saw me, and he stopped without any*
> *trace of alarm; over the spangled grass we stared at each*
> *other. ...And then, it was as if all the chains of a kind of*
> *slavery dropped from me with such a rush that they tin-*
> *kled and rattled in my imagination. Suddenly, I had fin-*
> *ished with the war, and a great rush of emotion swept*
> *over me that was impossible to describe except that all its*
> *urges and manifestations met in a wordless cry 'I have*
> *come home!'*

One can appreciate the profound healing that occurred in this peak experience described by Van der Post. Words cannot fully describe the power of it, as is the case with most significant mystical events. The fact that it occurred in nature is relevant to the power that nature has to move this energy within us and to heal us. Healing is occurring at the deepest level of existence. It is vitally clear in van der Post's description that, in that moment in time, he and the kudu bull were one and that this unity consciousness was expressed in the statement, "I have come home!"

It is not unusual to encounter an animal in the wild and for a brief moment fuse with it because one is in an altered state of consciousness. It is here that the animal, the wilderness trekker, and the process of observing can all become one experience. Native Americans were keenly aware that when one is in nature for extended periods with the right intent this could occur. This animal would then become a totem of power to that particular individual and a sign that he could be assisted in his life's quest by the qualities of that animal.

The key to moving the Kundalini energy upward is the balance of the female and male energies, the Ida and the Pingala, the cool moon and the hot sun. This bears a strong resemblance to the Western psychological approach we have already discussed in facilitating the inward, or transcendent, journey in wilderness by the balancing of the right brain (feminine) and left brain (masculine) to achieve a whole brain experience.

In yoga the word *Hatha* describes it well. *Ha* is the sun and *Tha* is the moon. Yoga represents balance of these two principles. Hatha yoga also means forceful yoga, the doctrine that practices perfecting the body as a means of self-realization.

⤳

T HE CHAKRA MODEL IS NOT dissimilar to Maslow's hierarchy of needs. The lowermost three chakras fulfill his descriptions of Deficiency needs. Only when these have been fulfilled can attention be directed to the Growth-oriented needs. Deficiency needs are related to stability, security, protection, and procreation, and only once these are satisfied can Growth needs be invoked. The Deficiency needs are reflected in the qualities of the first three chakras below the diaphragm and Growth needs by those found in the higher chakras above. If Deficiency needs become over emphasized and distorted as the only reality, this can block progress toward self-actualization.

Maslow's Growth needs involve qualities such as love, self-esteem, aliveness, justice, and truth. The highest of these needs are self-actualization followed by self-transcendence. It is in this realm that he described the mystical event or peak experience. Here, the individual transcends to clarity, euphoria, holism, and understanding, coming closer to the true self and a sense of his or her own being. It seems likely, looking at the similarities between the two systems, that Maslow's thinking was influenced by the yoga model because he was familiar with Eastern philosophies. As Westerners we know that only once our Deficiency needs have been taken care of are we able to enter the inward journey without reservation.

In Maslow's hierarchy, self-esteem and self-sufficiency are just above love and belongingness and it is on these former qualities that Outward Bound and similar organizations concentrate. In fact they use the mastery of our base, deficiency, survival needs on the lower rungs of the ladder as a means of growing toward self-competence. This can lead to self-awareness, and it is self-awareness that helps us understand the limitations of ego and enables us to ascend the hierarchy or go beyond the third to the higher chakras.

⤳

WHEN ONE THINKS OF HEALING, one looks to the healing profession and to the physician whose symbol is the caduceus. Hermes was the messenger of the gods and the patron of heralds. He carried a gold caduceus given to him by Apollo when they became friends. The caduceus is a staff around which two serpents are intertwined and at its top is a pair of wings. In Greek mythology this staff was a sign of power like the scepter of kings. The heads of the two serpents coming together signified talk of negotiations after warfare had ended, and the wings, the speed of the herald or messenger.

If one looks at the caduceus it is not difficult to see the exact replica of the chakra system and the three main nadis (the Ida, Pingala, and Sushumna; the left; the right, and the central column). Each one of the serpents winding around Herme's staff can be thought of as representative of the Ida and Pingala. The staff itself represents the central column, or the Sushumna. Furthermore, each serpent embraces the central staff in five places, representing the first five chakras. Where the serpents eye each other is the sixth chakra. The sixth chakra is where Ida and Pingala end before deviating to their respective nostrils. The crown or seventh chakra is represented by the wings and the head at the top of the staff. The wings, rather than signifying the speed of the messenger, seem symbolic of the seventh chakra, the thousand-petaled lotus in yoga, which exists four fingers above the crown and is the place of bliss consciousness whose manifestation is

THE CADUCEUS.

pure light. The connection between the archetypal serpents of the caduceus and the chakra system is striking.

Hermes represented many of the facets of the light and the dark. He was a complex figure who was a wanderer and bringer of luck, but also a thief with an astute mind. He became the god of herds and shepherds and could tell the future by lots. He therefore was in control of his third eye or sixth chakra. He made the first lyre and gave it to Apollo as compensation for the cattle he had stolen from him. This creative musical talent indicates that his right-brain activity was fully functional. Apollo, in gratitude, made him chief herald, giving him the gold staff. Hermes also was the god of fertility and luck, closely associated with the earth. He was a symbol for individuation because he was a master at balancing the light and the dark: the right and left, the Ida and the Pingala, the feminine and the masculine.

Unfortunately the medical profession chose Aesculapius (or Aesclepius) as its symbol—a staff with only one snake winding around it. To me this signifies the direction the profession has taken, one of reliance on the left brain and an attempt to make medicine a pure science rather than the healing art it is. We have forgotten the more feminine, compassionate, intuitive polarity represented by the second snake on the caduceus.

Physicians are offended by Hermes because he embodies some of the aspects of the dark side. However, we need to understand that our shadow side is a vital part of our being and it is through the shadow that we can come to understand the light. We need the right as well as the left, the dark as well as the light. The message of the caduceus embodies the same core belief of the balance of opposites that has relevance not only to self-healing and the wilderness effect but to any of the challenges we undertake during life's journey.

⸎

> *The Kundalini in the form of latency is coiled like a ser-*
> *pent. One who impels this Shakti to move will attain*
> *liberation.*
>
> Hatha Yoga, Pradipika

I T WAS FELT BY THE yogis that all that exists in the universe also exists in the human body—as is the macrocosm, so is the microcosm. By recognizing the truth of the human body and our own selves, we can come to recognize the truth of nature and the entire universe. Kundalini is felt to be female energy, or Shakti, existing in latent form, not only in every human being but in every atom of the universe. The purpose of Kundalini Yoga is to awaken this cosmic energy and unite Shakti with Shiva to attain pure consciousness, which is the same consciousness that pervades the whole cosmos. It is felt that every spiritual experience is related to the unfolding of this energy. When pure consciousness or bliss consciousness occurs, all sense of duality disappears and unity consciousness results. In this way the truth of the experience can be extrapolated to the truth embodied in the entire universe.

Bija or seed sounds are primordial sounds that are extremely important for arousing the Kundalini energy. The complex chants used by the Kalahari San in their healing ceremonies probably incorporate all of these primordial sounds. They seem to be a sophisticated, orchestrated rendition of the bush mantra heard when one listens to the magical non-human voices of the Kalahari night. The Kundalini is thought to be the origin of primordial sound as no doubt is nature herself.

The basic mechanism of the Kundalini experience is an increase in vibrational energy perceived as heat. As Kundalini rises up the spine from one chakra to the next, the vibration or volatility increases. In this way, the solidity of earth can become the liquidity of water, which then can become gaseous, air-like, and finally ether-like. This change from earth to water to fire to air to ether, or solid to liquid to gaseous to ether, occurs as Kundalini energy rises up from the first to the second to the third to the fourth and fifth chakras respectively. The Kalahari San also have represented this vibrational energy in their rock paintings as a series of zig-zag lines moving up the body. This profound change in energy—that must extend itself to every atom and every cell in the body—may be the secret to the adepts mastery of heat or cold. The Kundalini moves in a spiral and one could speculate that the spiral structure of the DNA molecule protects it from heat damage as the "vibration" of the cell approximates the "vibration" of fire.

Each chakra functions as a transformer and accelerates energy onward and upward to the next chakra. When the Kundalini energy rises all the way up the spine to the seventh chakra, the process is complete and the Kundalini can discharge itself, travel back down the spine to reside at the root chakra until its next awakening.

The trance dance or healing dance of the Kalahari Kung San is a Kundalini phenomenon. The only difference between the Bushmen experience and that of the yogis is a lack of sophisticated written language to describe it. The San experience is all the more remarkable because other than their attunement to the earth and cosmos and their delicate way of social interaction, they have no esoteric tradition to induce this state. Neither do they use psychedelics, except to help a neophyte having difficulties with the dance break into this advanced state of consciousness. Once the apprentice has made this shift, the catalyst is no longer used.

⤳

ONE OF THE QUALITIES OF Kundalini energy is the ability to control heat. Tibetan yogis are known to dry wet sheets on their naked bodies in the icy environment of the Tibetan mountains. Similarly, the Kalahari San can control fire and are able to place their body parts in flames or coals without being burned.

Another facet common to yogis and the San is the large-body experience. Here the person in trance travels out of body and, on looking down at his body on the earth, perceives it as being huge or elongated. This experience has been rendered beautifully on rock surfaces by San artists over the ages.

One aspect of Tantra Yoga is the belief that we rise by that which we fall. Sexual energy is felt to have enormous potential, and the energy of sex can be raised to a higher level of awareness. Maslow acknowledged that sex was one of the most powerful means to induce a peak experience. In Tantra the sexual union of male and female energies simulates the mystical union of Shiva and Shakti. As the male and female embrace one another, their individual egos dissolve leading to transcendence. Now there is no difference between the two, and the male and female, Shiva and Shakti, are one with the universe. In this way peak experiences or deep emotional connections can occur during sexual intercourse. The energy of Shakti embraces the archetype of the Earth Mother.

In the context of wilderness rapture, where the spiritual benefits of nature can range from a simple feeling of calmness and harmony to a profound mystical peak experience, it is useful to put the experience in the context of an energy model. Rather than say "Show me the Kundalini and I will believe it exists," it is valuable to appreciate this dynamic to experience its energy, either in subtle or profound form. Some other manifestations of Kundalini are outlined in the Table 2 (following page).

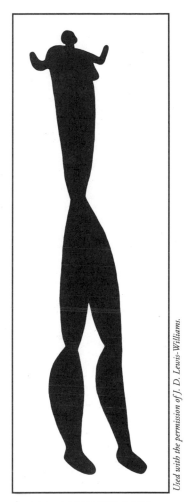

Used with the permission of J. D. Lewis-Williams.

A LARGE-BODY EXPERIENCE.

Tribal rock art depicts how a person traveling out of body will look back at his body and perceive it as huge and elongated.

EXPRESSIONS OF KUNDALINI

Heat rising up the spine.

Mastery of fire.

Creeping sensations; tingling.

Trembling.

Paralysis—falling.

Spontaneous movements.

Light experiences; inner sounds; smells of perfumes.

An empty mind.

Paranormal powers; intuitive knowledge.

Out-of-body experiences.

Large-body experience.

TABLE 2.

Kia, the phenomenon that occurs in the trance dance of the Kalahari Kung San, has been described by Richard Katz in his book, *Boiling Energy*. This book discusses most facets of the trance dance, which bears close resemblance to the Kundalini experience of the yogis and similar experiences described in other cultures. The event is induced by clapping, singing, chanting, and dancing around a fire. Usually, it is the men who dance around the fire while the women generate the energy of the dance with their clapping, singing, and chanting. An older woman often tends the fire. In addition, the rhythm of the dance is facilitated by the use of rattles wound around the dancers' legs.

The dance is primarily a healing ceremony for individuals who are ill and for the group as a whole, where it diffuses tensions that tend to accumulate. By connecting with the ancestral spirits, the lesser gods and the Great Spirit as well, paranormal information is made available to the shamans to assist in the healing. The shaman cannot approach the spirit world unless in this altered state of consciousness.

Num appears to be the San equivalent of the potential energy that lies dormant at the base of the spine, the Kundalini energy. During the dance the energy intensifies as the singing and clapping become more intense. The dancers may become stiff or rubbery and may stagger, shiver, shake, or fall. Often the dancer convulses in pain and screams. The healer goes to each person, lays on hands over the back and chest, pulls out the sickness, and shakes his hands toward the heavens, casting out the illness into the darkness. The dancers sweat profusely and may have a blank or glassy stare when all thought becomes suspended. Fear is a large part of the experience, both from pain as well as the encounter with the unknown. The healer entreats and argues with the gods and spirits for the patient's health.

The San believe that Num was given to the Kung San by the gods. Those who can heal possess Num, which resides in the pit of the stomach (in the Taoist tradition, the Hara, the origin of the vital force chi), and at the base of the spine (in the yoga tradition the seat of Kundalini power). Num heats up and becomes a vapor, a description identical to that of the yoga tradition. Num then rises up the spine to the base of the skull where Kia occurs and the healer travels out of body to the spirit realm on behalf of the patient.

Used with the permission of Dr. Aron D. Mazel.

NUM ENERGY.

This piece of San rock art shows vibrational num energy rising through the healer during a trance dance.

Kia seems to be the yoga equivalent of Shakti meeting Shiva at the crown chakra. As this vibrational energy rises up the spinal column, the spine tingles. According to one shaman's description to Katz: "Num makes your thoughts nothing in your head." With Kia, one could see into people and diagnose the illness. One could also leave the body to visit family members far away and to scout game. Immunity from the harmful effects of fire were part of the power of Num and Kia.

Num songs stimulate Num and open the healer's heart. Most likely they contain all the qualities of primordial sound so important in yoga for balancing and stimulating the chakras and nadis. The chanting, singing, and clapping are unique and, in the context of the Kalahari night and the flickering primal fire, have tremendous power. The yogis knew that these primordial sounds activated the Kundalini, and San healers are well aware of the importance of women in generating the energy of the dance with this form of sound. Comparisons between the yoga and San experience are outlined in the Table 3.

COMPARISON OF KUNDALINI AND KIA

Kundalini	Kia
The serpent power residing at the base of the spine, which can rise up to the crown and cause ecstasy.	The trance experience of the Kung San. An out-of-body experience where Num energy rises up the spine and comes out of the top of the head.
A mystical event that helps attain self-realization.	Used for healing and harmonizing the group.
Three knots must be pierced. The heart is the hardest.	To Kia, the heart must be open for Kundalini to rise.

TABLE 3. *Continued on page 145.*

Kundalini	Kia
Attained by Patanjali's eight-limbed yoga.	Induced by clapping, singing, dancing, chanting, rattles, and the primal fire.
Herbs used by the guru to facilitate the process.	Num plants used to help the initiate enter trance.
Shakti meets Shiva above the crown chakra.	The soul leaves out of the top of the head.
Magical powers can be a hindrance to personal growth.	Paranormal powers help the group (to hunt).
Dietary taboos essential. They are vegatarians.	Avoidance of meat only temporary.
Can induce in disciples by energy transference.	Teacher can induce Kia by shooting invisible arrows.
Resides at the base of the spine.	Resides at the base of the spine and the pit of the stomach.
The yogi attains god-consciousness in Samadhi (bliss).	The shaman will only enter the spirit world in (the state of) Kia.
Numerous old texts on how to to move Kundalini energy.	Handed on by oral tradition.
Advanced yogis attain it effortlessly.	Experienced shamans can Kia easily with more control and effective healing.
Primordial sounds facilitate the process.	Num songs are critical.
Part of recorded history.	May go back 40,000 years or more, as depicted in early rock art.

TABLE 3. *Continued from previous page.*

The Bushmen agree that male Num and female Num are the same. The female equivalent of Kia is more controlled and less dramatic. Trembling is a key component of it. Whereas males require a long period of learning and it is difficult for them to Kia, females could acquire Num and Kia in a few days. Any female who wanted Num was believed to be able to get it. However, pregnancy interrupted Num and a female could not concentrate on healing until the child-bearing years were over. It was for this reason that more males were healers than females. With most, the power would leave as one became older; however, in some females it remained and became even stronger. It was thought that females often had the strongest Num and this might develop as they became menopausal.

Descriptions of the trance dance given to Katz by healers included a feeling of unfolding, unwinding, untying oneself, spreading oneself apart or feeling oneself again. Num was felt to make your heart sweet. All of these have some of the attributes of a peak experience and of Samadhi, or bliss or unity consciousness. Similarly, in Kabbalah the highest sephira, Keter the crown, is the place of "I am that I am."

A vital quality of the healers was that they were able to tap into the right brain function more easily. In other words, they were more in touch with the feminine side of brain activity. Katz described this as being more emotionally labile, more expressive and passionate, and having a body image or self-image that was more determined by inner states than by anatomy. He felt they had easy access to a rich fantasy life and that they were more intuitive than they were logical. Possibly this is the reason that the women were able to trance more easily than the men; they required only a brief apprenticeship and often were the best healers.

This transcendent ability of the San seems at least in part related to their close connection with wilderness and all the facilitative properties it possesses. The fact that, unlike the hunter-gatherers of the Amazon, they do this without hallucinogens is all the more remarkable. For those of us interested in the multifaceted experience of nature, there can be no better model for us than the hunter-gatherers and especially the San. We can aspire not only to their technical expertise in the wild, or the so-called "hard skills" but also to their advanced mystical and magical abilities that arise out of the softer approach of tapping into the feminine dimension not only of themselves but also of the Earth Mother and the cosmos.

∽

FURTHER READING

Brennan, Barbara Ann. *Hands of Light: A Guide to Healing Through the Human Energy Field.* (Summary of work by Valery Hunt, UCLA 1977, and Dr. Hiroshi Montoyama, Tokyo, Japan, I.A.R.P., 1979.) New York: Bantam Books, 1987.

Feuerstein, Georg. *The Encyclopedic Dictionary of Yoga.* New York: Paragon House, 1990.

Feuerstein, Georg. *Yoga: The Technology of Ecstasy.* Los Angeles: Jeremy P. Tarcher Inc., 1989.

Gerber, Richard, M.D. *Vibrational Medicine.* Santa Fe, New Mexico: Bear & Company, 1988. Chapter 4 is a summary of work by Montoyama and Bentov.

Grof, Christina and Stanislav Grof. *The Stormy Search for the Self.* Los Angeles: Jeremy P. Tarcher Inc., 1990.

Grof, Stanislav and Christina Grof. *Spiritual Emergency.* Los Angeles: Jeremy P. Tarcher Inc., 1989.

Hunt, Valery, et al. *Abstract. A Study of Structural Integration from Neuromuscular, Energy Field and Emotional Approaches,* Sponsored by the Rolf Institute of Structural Integration, 1977.

Johari, Harish. *Chakras: Energy Centers of Transformation.* Rochester, Vermont: Destiny Books, 1987.

Katz, Richard. *Boiling Energy: Community Healing Among the Kalahari Kung.* Cambridge, Massachusetts: Harvard University Press, 1982.

Krishna, Gopi. *Kundalini, the Evolutionary Energy in Man.* Boston: Shambhala, 1985.

Maslow, A. H. *The Farther Reaches of Human Nature.* New York: Penguin, 1976.

Mookerjee, Ajit. *Kundalini, the Arousal of Inner Energy.* London: Thames and Hudson, 1989.

Muktananda, Swami. *Play of Consciousness.* San Francisco: Harper & Row, 1978.

N. E. Thing Enterprises. *Magic Eye II: 3-D Illusions.* Kansas City: Andrews and McMeel, 1994.

Sandweiss, Samuel H., M.D. *Sai Baba the Holy Man...and the Psychiatrist.* San Diego: Birth Day Publishing Company, 1975.

Sannella, Lee, M.D. *The Kundalini Experience.* Lower Lake, California: Integral Publishing, 1987.

CHAPTER TEN

KABBALAH, THE TREE OF LIFE, AND OTHER CORE TRUTHS

*It is a Tree of Life to those who hold it fast, and all who
cling to it find happiness. Its ways are ways of pleasantness
and all its paths are peace.*

Maimonides

K ABBALAH IS THE JEWISH MYSTICAL tradition and has characteristics that
can be compared to those found in yoga and, to some of the ecstatic
states, of the San. Tthe language of the Kabbalah is universal and archetypal. It contains a core belief of opposites, as well as other principles of
spiritual truth that are found in many traditions.

If we are to connect with our inner being in or outside of nature, a reaf-
firmation of these principles can help us on our quest. Furthermore our
spiritual relationship with nature is so complex that the more models we
explore the greater will be our understanding of wilderness rapture. The
Kabbalistic Tree of Life is an ancient archetype and is symbolic not only of
our relationship with the transcendent, but also with our connection to the
Earth Mother as well. It is another map to look at as we explore the topog-
raphy of ourselves in and outside of nature. The Tree is our link between
heaven and earth and is a good metaphor for the inward bound journey
that also seeks to link the two.

The Tree of Life is composed of three limbs and three principles. These
three principles are represented in the three vertical parts of the tree. On
the left is rigor, severity, passive force, and constraint or constriction; on the
right, mercy, active force, and expansion; and in the middle, main trunk of
the tree, equilibrium, grace, and will, which hold the balance.

The tree is composed of ten sephirot and twenty-two pathways between
the sephirot. These sephirot are in some ways analogous to the chakras in
yoga and represent centers of force or energy. The crown or topmost

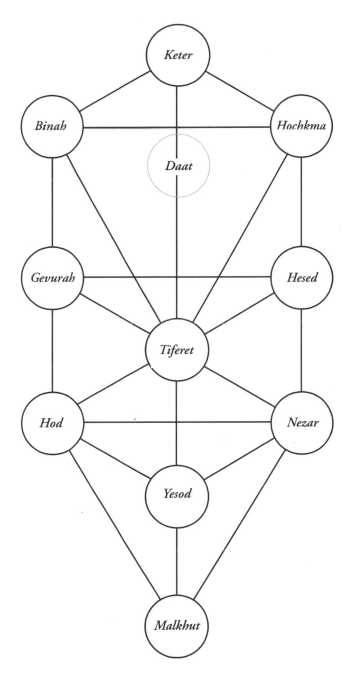

THE KABBALISTIC TREE OF LIFE.

In the beginning, before the serpent tempts Eve to eat of the Tree of Knowledge and Adam follows suit, the two of them are living in a state of naive bliss with everything provided by the garden. They are the same as children who, in their simplicity, are pure and have not yet developed their ego sense—their third chakra—or the sephira of Yesod. Knowledge of the fruit changes this dramatically, and they first become aware of their nudity. After they cover themselves and hide from God, God challenges them with their crime, the punishment of which is that woman will suffer the pain of childbirth and will be dominated by man. Man will till the soil and from that time on.

> *...Cursed is the ground for thy sake; in toil shalt thou eat of it all the days of thy life...in the sweat of thy face shalt thou eat bread till thou return unto the ground....*

> Genesis 3:17

This description has changed little up to the present day and is symbolic of our being bound to the power of ego, which demands we make our way in the world in a physical and materialistic way. It is only the true hunter-gatherer who may have escaped this sentence and lives in relative bliss off the Earth Mother. Statistics have shown that hunter-gatherers like the San are blessed with more leisure time than we could ever dream of having. Recently, however, this has been changing as the few hunter-gatherers left are rapidly run out of their gardens of Eden. Even those who have a small place left in the garden have eaten of the fruit of the Tree of Knowledge, which can be thought of as representing the ego creating the monster of consumerism and materialism. In their innocent-like state, the hunter-gatherers are even less capable than we are of integrating the wonders of modern-day living into their daily lives and usually end up consuming the one thing they can barely afford—alcohol. This, as Carl Jung pointed out, is another, though unfortunate way of connecting with "spirit."

God also placed another tree in the Garden of Eden, the Tree of Life. We are still able to return to Eden by embarking on a journey up this tree. Just as we came down the tree as a lightning flash to become manifest in human form at the sephira of Malkhut, we have the option of doing the lightning flash in reverse by controlling the serpent wound around the trunk of the tree, transcending the ego of Yesod, and reaching the higher sephirot beginning with Tiferet. With devotion we may even reach Keter, at which point we can enter Eden again in a state of Yehud, or unity consciousness and bliss, recognizing as before that "I am that I am," as we connect with our divine self made in the image of God.

> *And the Lord said; Behold the man is become as one of us, to know good and evil; and now lest he put forth his hand and take also of the Tree of Life and live and eat forever. Therefore, the Lord God sent him forth from the garden of Eden to till the ground from whence he was taken. So he drove out the man; and he placed at the east of the garden of Eden the cherubim and the flaming sword which turned every way, to keep the way to the Tree of Life.*

> Genesis 3:22

ᔐ

ON OUR WILDERNESS QUEST WE can enter the garden again and by our practice win over the cherubim so that they lay aside their flaming swords and allow us to regain our birthright, which is access to our divine nature. For some of us that do not ascribe to any religious philosophy, this can most easily be done in the context of nature herself rather than through any austere esoteric tradition, as long as we learn the principles these paths have to teach us. We can use these tenets as tools to help us on the journey rather than as a set belief to adhere to. In addition we can use the hunter-gatherers as our model because they embrace many of these principles and until recently were still the closest to the Garden of Eden experience. The principles they embody are a humble demeanor or lack of ego, lack of judgment in the group, unconditional love for their children, minimal attachment to the material, and being in the present moment with themselves and their environment.

The only way back in, is the way we were driven out. We have to embark on a long and arduous journey to realize again what we once had, or, as T. S. Eliot said so eloquently, "We shall not cease from exploration and the end of all our exploring will be to arrive where we started and know the place for the first time."

On the other hand we have an advantage over the San in that we left the garden long ago and have had more opportunity to wend our way back. The San are only now beginning their difficult trek out and their trail leader is the ego. They have a long way to go until they understand the complications caused by this new leadership and recognize what they left behind.

Tiferet, the heart of the Tree, and the equivalent of the heart chakra, represents self-awareness and it is at Tiferet that one can stop spiritual growth and remain in the materialism that exists below this sephira. One can have comfort, power, and prestige, but no propensity for spiritual growth. In yoga the equivalent would be focusing all energy in the lower three chakras below the diaphragm. According to Maslow, this would be the same as never growing beyond our Deficiency needs.

Kabbalah affirms that our desire is to return to Eden from whence we came. This is the equivalent of the search for the higher self of the yogis, or self-realization. Ancient Kabbalistic drawings of the Tree of Life reveal a serpent coiled around the pillar of equilibrium. According to Kabbalah, the hero must conquer the serpent coiled around the central trunk of the tree in order to attain Keter or enlightenment. Kabbalah, like other ancient traditions, describes its own archetypal journey of the hero; and the serpent coiled around the central trunk can be compared to the Kundalini serpent coiled around the Sushumna nadi blocking the flow of spiritual energy with its tail in its mouth. The snake or ego was our downfall but conquering it can be our salvation.

IT IS NOT DIFFICULT TO find similar mystical and spiritual qualities throughout yoga, Kabbalah, and the San hunter-gatherers. We can use these qualities to augment and facilitate our spiritual adventure in the wild outdoors. If we were to look at one environment that is multi-factorial and provides the maximum number of benefits one would require for self-discovery, the choice would have to be nature or wilderness. Here one can easily connect with the four elements. Earth, water, fire, and air are close at hand; when you need them for survival they take on a different significance. We are able to master the first chakra if we spend enough time in nature, where we can experience the flight or fight reaction in its true form, rather than in the way we are accustomed to dealing with it in modern day life, as a state of chronic, low grade panic.

In the wild, we can recognize our power base and our ego strength in the third chakra, or in the sephira of Yesod and exposure to its challenges provides an excellent tool for gaining self-mastery and self-esteem. It is likely that if we can raise the energy above Yesod or above the diaphragm to the higher centers we can come to know our place of truth in the universe; the Hebrew word for which is Tikun.

If we are to make use of some of the principles of ancient traditions in wilderness, the key factor we can distill out of the mass of information available, is the concept of a core belief or universal truth. This core belief permeates all the different disciplines: right brain-left brain, Ida-Pingala, Ha-Tha, Ying-Yang, contraction-expansion, light-dark. We are able to recognize and appreciate a plethora of opposites in nature and the wild outdoors and it is in balancing these that we come to find our own center.

San and Bantu healers in Southern Africa make use of bones for divining and one can discern the same principles of polarity and balance we have seen in other mystical traditions. There are bones for male and female, strong and weak, black and white, fast and slow.

Eduardo Calderon, the Peruvian shaman, worked by balancing good and evil which he did from the base of his Mesa (table). On top of the Mesa power objects were laid out in a set pattern. The good artifacts were on the right, or the light side; the evil were on the left, or the dark side; and the middle field was the mediating center between them. Many of the northern Peruvian shamans seem to work through the same principle of balancing

CALDERON'S MESA.

the two forces. This balancing of opposites is archetypal and translates into an essential conviction that is universal. It is also more true to the symbolism of the caduceus than is modern-day medicine, which concentrates on the left or cognitive to the exclusion of the right or intuitive.

Eduardo explains further that the field to the right is the field of justice, and the one to the left is the field of evil. The field of justice is where Christ and all his saints dwell; Christ is the main force that erases all negative influences. The field of evil contains all the negative forces, and one must look here for the cause of the problem. This may occur as a result of sorcery or a natural malady. Depending on which it is, a different power object on the left side of the Mesa will vibrate, and this vibration can be identified only when the shaman is in an altered state of consciousness, with the third eye opened by a potion containing, among other plants, the hallucinogen mescaline found in the San Pedro cactus. One can make a diagnosis with the help of San Pedro, and the treatment for the problem also is made available to the healer with the help of San Pedro. In the center of the Mesa is the mediating center, which balances the opposing fields and is responsible for the balance of the Mesa.

It is significant that the San Pedro cactus blooms at night and, therefore, it is at night that one uses the power of the plant and its vital energy. Among the San the healing or trance dance also stops shortly after dawn. The San involve themselves in all-night rituals, especially during the summer months when the weather is warm. It would be difficult to believe that these ceremonies could hold as much power if done outside of nature and without the tools she is able to provide the shaman.

⤳

THE CANDELABRA OR TRIDENT NEAR Paracas in southern coastal Peru has strong similarities to the Tree of Life. The Trident, which is etched on a hill in the desert sands, resembles a huge cactus. It is a massive figure, 600 feet long and 200 feet wide, and has changed little in hundreds of years. Some scientists have linked it to the Southern Cross constellation. Erik von Daniken speculated that it was a sign for extraterrestrial spacecraft and pointed the way toward the enigmatic Nazca lines further south. However, an extraterrestrial using it as a beacon would miss the lines by 150 miles.

The Candelabra is an archetypal cactus-like figure with three limbs like the Kabbalistic Tree of Life. The balance between the left and right limbs of the cactus leads to integration that is the key to knowledge and self-realization. This occurs when one reaches the top of the central column of the trident. This cactus-like figure can also reminds us of the properties inherent in the San Pedro cactus that have helped shamans access the supernatural for millennia.

There is another fascinating figure in the Nazca sands south of Paracas called The Needle and Thread. It is a quarter of a mile in length and consists

THE CANDELABRA OR TRIDENT OF PERU.

THE NEEDLE AND THREAD.

A schematic drawing of the figure in the Nazca sands of Peru.

Paul Cumes

of a central column and a zigzag line that crosses it sixteen times. The figure has a spiral at its base from which the zigzag leads. The zigzag crisscrosses the column as it travels up, and ends at the pinnacle of the column. It can return down the axis of the column to join the spiral again. At first sight the figure looks very mysterious, but it does not take a lot of imagination to find similarities between this and the chakra system or even the lightning bolt of the Kabbalistic Tree. The spiral could represent potential energy waiting to be discharged, much the same as the Kundalini serpent is coiled in the central column of the Sushumna. The zigzag line symbolically is the same as the flow of this force up the spinal column and has been depicted in similar fashion by the San in their rock art.

ALTHOUGH THERE ARE DIFFERENCES CROSS culturally in the symbolism, the deeper meaning of the process is the same. In one way or another, energy is moved upward by various esoteric practices and techniques. To the yogi it is Kundalini Shakti meeting Shiva at the crown chakra in Samadhi. To the Kabbalist it is the path up the Tree of Life to Keter. To the San shaman it is Num rising up the spine and blowing out the base of the skull with Kia. To the desert shaman of Peru, the dynamic is depicted by The Needle and Thread and also the Trident or Candelabra, which so much resembles the Tree of Life.

Wilderness rapture is profound, and we are able to understand this better if we look to these wonderful examples of wilderness art arising out of the original nature religions. There are examples of rock art left by the ancients all over the planet. If we encounter them on our sojourns into wilderness, an appreciation of the powerful forces leading to their inspiration and manifestation can help us in our own meditations when we visit these areas of sacred space.

Some of the San rock art in Southern Africa showing different aspects of the trance dance and trance-like states can be dated back 40,000 years, and it is clear that these spiritual practices must predate the recordings in ancient yoga scriptures or those written down by the Jewish mystics. Just as humanity began in Africa, it might be that the Southern African continent was the place of sophisticated psycho-spiritual technology long before God made a covenant with Abraham, or the yogis began to practice eight-limbed yoga. These practices may have facilitated the formation of mystical roots in other traditions beyond the so-called "dark" continent. They also arose in the context of nature and the Earth Mother, and if we are to reconnect intimately with this power it is useful to learn from the wisdom of the past. We cannot separate our experience in the wild from the inherent qualities invoked by nature's ability to move the spirit within us. No doubt if we spent all our time in wilderness we would need an outlet for this overwhelming feeling of oneness; and if we had no conventional art technology, we would want to express our transcendent experiences somewhere on the parchment of the earth's crust with the tools and dyes provided by the wild.

Because few of us can live permanently and intimately in the wild outdoors, if we want to facilitate her healing energy we need to contrive an effective, even if not spontaneous strategy to maximize our retreat.

One participant in a workshop I once gave was somewhat concerned about the "recipe" I was giving for touching the transcendent within us. I prefer to look at it as the understanding of a certain dynamic with which each of us can then do what we like. The most important principle is to try and remove our old conditioning so that nature can get on with the job of healing us. In any event the effect will never be predictable and all we need is a way to open ourselves up to all possibilities.

The Bhagavad-Gita says: "Whatever being comes to be, be it motionless or moving, derives its being from the union of Field, and Knower of the Field; know this!" The more we can know about the field of nature, the cosmos, and about ourselves, the better.

Whenever we can on trail, we enlist the help of a local shaman to give us an extra dimension to the nature spirit world we are about to enter. He or she not only protects us on our journey but also gives us insights into the subtle forces that surround us.

In a Western sense, we can balance left- and right-brain activity and attain "whole" brain function. For those who are more left-brained in inclination, we can concentrate more on right brain stimuli such as those obtained during soft skills and soft fascinations. By paying attention to the Kung San we can make full use of primordial sound, singing, dancing, chanting, clapping, the primal fire, and their enlightened social interaction. The chakra system of the yogis can help us appreciate that we have a sophisticated energy body not described in conventional, anatomical, and physiological texts that we can stimulate and balance with the use of different esoteric techniques. These do not have to be bizarre or extraordinary, but certainly breath work and meditation are easily in reach of most Westerners.

The Kabbalists have given us the Tree of Life with its emphasis on wisdom, understanding, knowledge, mercy, and justice. Kabbalah, like all ancient traditions, rests on a firm, moral foundation and incorporates many of the properties described in the yoga tradition of chakras and Kundalini. With some of this knowledge it is likely that we will be able to amplify, magnify, and facilitate our own wilderness experience and take it to new depths and greater heights. Some knowledge of these ancient wisdoms that understood the mechanism of transcendence can be of great assistance to us on our inner journey into nature and into our own inner wilderness.

Again, leisure time in nature mixed with non-directed attention for soft fascinations can facilitate this process. If we can relate to the heart, the fourth chakra, with compassion, empathy, and love, we will more easily be able to gain access to the fifth chakra and express ourselves through song, dance, writing, poetry, or any other form of artistic expression. In the Kabbalistic sense we will have reached Tipheret.

The San of old were prolific painters and their sacred wilderness art is all over the rock faces of Southern Africa. Their intimate connection with the Mother Earth and the cosmos gave them access to these higher chakras, including the third eye, or sixth chakra, which they used for intuitive and paranormal knowledge. Many San still can obtain access to the seventh—the crown chakra—by using the technique of trance dancing or Kia. One can still witness this phenomenon today in the Kalahari Desert. Music and the primordial sound of Num songs provide the San with an easy vehicle

FURTHER READING

Bentov, Itzhak. *Stalking the Wild Pendulum*. Bantam Books, 1981.

Calderon, Eduardo, Richard Cowan, Douglas Sharon, and F. Kaye Sharon. *Eduardo el Curandero: The Words of a Peruvian Healer*. Richmond, Louisiana: North Atlantic Books, 1982.

Devereaux, Paul. *Shamanism and the Mystery Lines*. St. Paul, Minnesota: Llewellyn Publications, 1993.

Dowson, Thomas A. *Rock Engravings of Southern Africa*. Johannesburg: Witwatersrand University Press, 1992.

Epstein, Pearl. *Kabbalah, the Way of the Jewish Mystic*. New York: Shambhala, 1972.

Graham, Rae. *Tales of the African Life*. Cape Town, South Africa: Struck Books, 1992.

Hadingham, Evan. *Lines to the Mountain Gods*. New York: Random House, 1987.

Halevi, Zev ben Shimon. *Kabbalah, Tradition of Hidden Knowledge*. London: Thames and Hudson, 1992.

Hammond-Tooke, David. *Rituals and Medicines*. Capetown, South Africa: Creda Press, 1989.

Pentateuch and Haftorahs, from Genesis. Edited by Dr. J. H. Hertz. London: Soncino Press: 1981.

Williams, J. D. Lewis and T. A. Dowson. "The Signs of All Times, Entoptic Phenomena in Upper Paleolithic Art," *Current Anthropology*, volume 29, number 2, April 1988.

CHAPTER ELEVEN

OPENING

UP THE

HEART

We are all climbing toward the summit of our heart's desire. Should the other climber steal your sack and your purse and wax fat on the one and heavy on the other, you should pity him. The climbing will be harder for his flesh and the burden will make his way longer. And should you in your leanness see his flesh puffing upward, help him in a step; it will add to your swiftness.

Unknown

IF WE ARE TO MAKE the most of our inward bound wilderness trek or any other spiritual pursuit, we need a practical way to take some of these simple but arduous principles with us into the wild. We do not have to transform our journey into a religious or devotional exercise, but by being mindful, aware, and in the moment with our personal process, we can improve the quality of our leisure time for ourselves and our accompanying travelers.

In this new age, a term we often hear is unconditional love. This is a lofty ideal, and few of us will ever reach that level of spiritual development where we can truly love everyone. The San shaman must open up the heart to Kia, or reach the transcendent through the trance dance. Yogis say that of the three blocks or "knots" existent in the chakra system that prevent the flow of Kundalini energy the heart block is the most important. The symbol of the heart chakra is the hexagon, or the six-pointed star similar to the Seal of Solomon or Star of David and the symbol of the Sephira of Tiferet. The Kabbalists affirm that once one reaches Tiferet, students on the spiritual path can teach themselves.

Tiferet to the Kabbalist represents the heart of the Tree and is invested with the qualities of beauty and adornment.

In yoga, the six-pointed star signifies the heart chakra. This hexagon consists of two overlapping triangles pointing in opposite directions. The

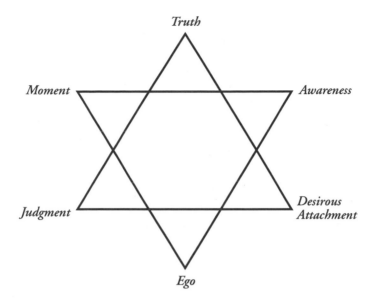

Truth

Moment

Awareness

Judgment

Desirous
Attachment

Ego

THE HEXAGON, SYMBOL OF THE HEART CHAKRA.

The three lower points indicate qualities of the three lower chakras below the diaphragm; the three upper points indicate qualities of those above the diaphragm.

apex of the triangle directed downward symbolizes the material descending to earth, and the apex of that pointing upward, the spiritual ascending to heaven. Also if one considers the heart as sitting on the top surface of the diaphragm, one can see how the three lowermost points of the six-pointed star indicate below the diaphragm while the three uppermost point upward.

The three lower points can be regarded as representing the spiritually inhibiting properties of the third chakra just below the diaphragm, namely judgment, attachment to objects of our desire (desirous attachment), and ego. The three upper points indicate three qualities of the upper chakras, namely truth, awareness, and being in the present moment. The hexagon itself embodies love, which is crucial for moving energy upward. A huge impediment to the flow of Kundalini energy resides in the third chakra and comprises ego, judgment, and desirous attachment. The diaphragm is essential for pranayama, the control of breath, and pranayama is one of the most important techniques used by the yogi to balance the two energies of Ida and Pingala, to get energy to move into the Sushumna and up into the higher chakras above the diaphragm. Not only does the diaphragm divide the lower from the higher chakras, but it is vital for raising energy into the heart chakra and up.

The true self lies beyond the ego and wilderness is one of the many practices available to subvert the ego on the way to the real self. Judgment and desirous attachment are powerful facilitators of the ego.

Buddha taught that our ego-grasping and self-cherishing behavior was not only the source of all our misery but also the biggest deterrent to reaching Nirvana and enlightenment. Only by doing things for their own sake rather than for an ego-based reason can we transform.

Judgment

> *Judge not, that ye be not judged. For with what judgment ye judge, ye shall be judged; and with what measure ye mete it shall be measured to you again.*
>
> Matthew 7:1–2

> *When you see a worthy person, endeavor to emulate him; when you see an unworthy person, then examine your inner self.*
>
> Confucius

What Confucius may have meant by this is that when we examine our inner selves in the space of judgment, we may find it truly wanting since there is no judgment in the place of true self; judgment occurs in the space of ego.

According to Sri Swami Rama: "Self condemnation strengthens guilt, which is one of the greatest obstacles on the path of realization."

This is why all spiritual traditions rest on a firm moral foundation and have tenets to reinforce righteous behavior. We cannot aspire to high ideals if we have a poor image of our character and behavior.

Furthermore, our own self-critical feeling that we are not good enough leads us to invest much energy into judging others to compensate for our feeling of deficiency. Judgment of others and of ourselves makes us angry and disturbs our equanimity. We suffer more from judging another than the person who is being judged.

Modern medical research has shown that people who are critical and easily angered are more prone to certain diseases. Therefore, if for no other reason than our own sakes, we need to try and suspend our tendency to find fault. Judgment also takes us out of the moment. If one is judging whether this is the best sunset one has ever seen, there is little energy left for being with the sunset. This space becomes occupied with the analysis of the event.

We spend much of our waking lives judging circumstances, situations, events, and people. When involved with this we are taken away from the nature of our higher self, since judgment reinforces our ego. Unfortunately, to be effective in the Western world, it is difficult to get rid of judgment entirely. We need to judge and evaluate others to see if they can do the job and if not, we eliminate them from our frame of reference. It would be more appropriate to use a softer word, like discernment, in this practical situation. On the inner journey into wilderness we can let personal judgment slide because there are no deadlines to meet and no goals to achieve. Similarly the San have a gentle pace of life and possibly this is why judgment is not a big part of their lives. When we go into the wilderness to encounter the true self, we need to release judgment because this can block the contact.

When there is peace, calm, and harmony, judgment falls aside. When there is no judgment, peace and calm result. It is like using breath for relaxation. Noticing and being aware of one's breathing puts us immediately in touch with our mood. If we are anxious or upset, our breathing is shallow and rapid; if we are calm and relaxed, then so is our breathing. We can control our state of mind by controlling our breathing. We can change a feeling of being upset and harried to one of being tranquil and at peace just by altering the breath. Similarly if we can control judgment, we can have a powerful effect on our spiritual progress.

We can forgive others their failings and idiosyncrasies if, at the same time, we forgive ourselves for something. We can make a trade: Forgive and let it go as we forgive ourselves for a failing we do not care for in our own personality. This barter system might work a little more effectively, since being non-judgmental in a situation that clearly evokes strong emotions can be extremely difficult.

On an intellectual level, we can look at the Indian medical system of Ayurveda. Ayurveda, which means the science of life, believes that people have a basic nature or Prakriti. Three main Doshas can make up someone's Prakriti: Vata, Pitta, and Kapha—each of which represents a mind-body type. This is more sophisticated than the simple Western definition of endo, meso, and ectomorph. Vata represents movement, Pitta metabolism, and Kapha structure. Following are some of their characteristics.

Vata people typically are thin, bony, and have tremendous energy. They are excitable, vivacious, and anxious; they exhaust easily if they overexert themselves. They are hyper-excitable and, true to their Vata principle of movement, they move about a lot. They grasp concepts quickly, but are quick to forget. When out of balance they tend to display anxiety and nervousness.

Pitta people represent the typical mesomorph and have more strength and endurance. They have excellent digestive capacity and cannot miss a meal without becoming ravenously hungry. They have sharp intellect, are enterprising, become angry with stress, take charge of situations, and are demanding, sarcastic, and critical.

Kapha people tend to be endomorphic and strong. They have steady energy, but tend to put on weight easily. They have compassion and empathy and are slow to anger. They tend to wake up slowly, improve their mood by eating, and have good retentive memories. They often remain attached to relationships and ideas.

We may have one or more qualities operating in our basic nature and are unable to change our makeup. If we try to be someone else and not true to our Dosha, we may go out of balance and eventually become diseased. Ayurveda gives many recommendations for keeping a particular Dosha in balance, by paying attention to whatever it is that gives our Dosha equilibrium. There is no such thing as a good or bad Dosha; the

Dosha just is. That is the way we are and it is the body-mind card we were dealt when we were born. Some of us are single Dosha types and others can be a mix of di- or tri-Dosha. It is the dominant Dosha that is likely to go out of balance. Of these, Vata is the most active and most likely to be the first affected adversely.

This excellent classification of mind-body type brings us insights into judgment. If we look at people in the light of their having a particular Dosha, we can forgive them more easily for some of their "faults." The over anxious, irritable Vata personality who has been excessively stressed, has not slept, and is exhausted no longer is seen as a jerk. We recognize these as signs of that person's Vata Dosha being out of balance. For Kapha personalities who have trouble getting up in the morning and constantly gain weight, we can appreciate their inherent Kapha nature instead of regarding them as lazy and undisciplined. By the same token, we can recognize some of our own behavior patterns and not judge ourselves so severely for our own deficiencies.

At the beginning of a trail, I introduce wilderness participants to this sophisticated mind-body classification so that we can all trek together more harmoniously in a non-judgmental way.

If all else fails we can remember the adage: "Whenever one points a finger there are three fingers pointing back at ourselves." We are incapable of recognizing a shadowy quality of someone else unless it is a part of our own shadow as well, and more often than not, judgment is a projection of our own shadow onto another. This fact is the guiding principal operating when the group is in the talking circle and no finger pointing is allowed.

Judgment can be positive or negative, and we are inclined to think that as long as we are saying good things no harm is done. Certainly praise is preferable to criticism, but it is still judgment. It has been my experience in the group setting that lavish praise can be just as harmful as strong condemnation. When we praise in a close-knit group, we compare one person's performance to the others, and this can lead to a feeling of inadequacy on behalf of those not being praised. It may be more constructive to the group as a whole to take the individual aside and say what must be said in private, be it appreciation or otherwise. Many of us find it difficult to talk about our own feelings and often remarks in the circle gravitate toward praise for one or other member of the group, the trip, the day, or the leaders themselves. Although it is easy and agreeable to listen to this type of contribution, it often distracts us from the main object of the circle, which is sharing more intimately a part of our inner self.

We may need to take another lesson from the San in this instance. They have sophisticated techniques of keeping everyone humble, which hold individual egos in check and maintain clan harmony and equanimity. Richard Lee, in his book *The Dobe Kung* describes what he has called "insulting the meat." This is an indifference or even a negativity displayed to the good news of a successful hunt by members of the clan. An accomplished hunter will tend to understate and be self-effacing and modest about what he has brought for the group, and the happy onlookers are more apt to say something derogatory about a kill. Even something as impressive as a giraffe may be met with a statement such as, "Do you expect this puny specimen will feed us all?" The hunter furthermore is expected to reply in an appropriate way; for example, "You are right, next time I will be luckier." This type of philosophy is vital in keeping the younger, more arrogant individuals in check.

The shadow archetype with its judgmental temperament is apt to come up in wilderness and can frequently be a disruptive force in the group. If the group has an understanding and awareness of the psychodynamics of this shady side of the ego self, each individual can take responsibility for his or her own shadow rather than assign blame and point fingers.

DESIRE AND ATTACHMENT

Buddha taught that all is sorrow, and desire that creates attachment is the main culprit for our suffering. Just as we can create inner calm by noticing our breath and achieve peace of mind by not judging others, we could prevent sorrow and suffering if we could stop our desirous attachments resulting from our ego-grasping nature. Desire and attachment are closely linked, as it is the desire for something that leads us to become attached to it. Desire without attachment can be quite healthy. It is ego that leads us to want and acquire "things," and through attachment prevents us from letting go.

In the wilderness we can come close to the hunter-gatherer model, since we are separated from home comforts, modern conveniences, and status symbols. In spite of this, many of us are still attached to the technology of our equipment, and conversations can easily gravitate around what kind of tent one has or how much one's boots cost. This takes on new significance in third world countries where the local help are doing well in sandals and short pants in situations where the rest of us in the same clothing would soon be hypothermic or frostbitten.

The San and most other hunter-gatherers own little and share everything. The Kung San also have a sophisticated system of gift exchange called Hxaro. Lee describes this as a delayed form of gift exchange, which is not necessarily equal in value. In this way goods circulate around the group and there is less chance of someone feeling deprived. The size or merit of the original gift bears no relationship to the size of the gift eventually returned. It is the thought and intent of the giving rather than its value that counts. The Kung San are more interested in the social interaction than the gift itself. Wealth was measured more by how many times one gave and exchanged than by how much one actually kept. Food and water are never exchanged, but freely given. Lee also stresses that gift exchange is a different process than barter. When I was in the Kalahari with a finite supply of food for my stay, I became very aware of my tendency to ration what I had. Although I would share food with the San at meal time, I realized that they could not understand why we did not just eat it all at once. Storing food or water is not in their mind frame.

The Quechua people of the Peruvian Andes have a similar system called Ayni. This means "Today for you, tomorrow for me." This system refers to a work exchange rather than a gift exchange. One day I help you till your fields, and on another you help me build my house. Again, the exchange does not have to be equivalent. The penalties of not reciprocating are severe and the culprit is likely to be ostracized from the community. However, no grudges are held and the moment reciprocation is instituted all is deemed well.

One of the advantages of trekking in exotic places is the knowledge one gains of local customs that can help us Westerners with our sometimes strained group interaction and trivial complaints. The trailist who is reluctant to share toilet paper can benefit from this exposure.

If we come back to Patanjali's Five Sheaths, particularly the Mind Sheath, we realize that these base emotions reside in the mind-body. Desires bubble up from the lower mind as do our emotions and habits relating to judgment. Judgment and desirous attachment are more a function of the mind-body and ego. Our intellectual body, or intellectual sheath, governs the mind-body; but in addition to this particular system of modulation we can replace these negative forces arising from "mind" with meditation, mantra (this can be the mantra of the sounds of the bush), and mindfulness. We cannot get rid of them, but we can become aware of how they control our lives, recognize them, and let them go. A regular spiritual practice of one form or another will help us on our way.

Because the inner journey into wilderness incorporates this principle and can become a profound meditation in itself, we can enjoy a sense of equanimity in nature and let go of our attachment not only to material objects but also to preconceived ideas and beliefs.

When we return to the essentials of what is involved in living in wilderness we can detach from desire, connect closely with the higher self, and let our judgments fall away. We need only emulate mother nature's neutral stance, since just as she does not judge us, we should not judge others.

Our pain creates judgment and physical pleasure augments desire, causing attachment to "things." If we can remain in the middle path, not becoming attached to pleasure or pain, judgment, or desire, our management of these difficult hurdles presented to us by the third chakra can be overcome and we can live more readily in the realm of the upper chakras.

The qualities of truth, awareness, and being in the present moment are represented in the upper chakras above the diaphragm. Each in turn occupies one of the points of the upper half of the hexagon of the heart chakra, which itself signifies love.

Truth is an integral part not only of the trek itself but also is manifest in the talking or council circle where the group shares feelings, insights, thoughts, and experiences in a milieu of honesty, trust, and openness. The talking circle is one of the most vital components of this inner journey and is an entire subject on its own. (*The Way of Council,* by Jack Zimmerman and Virginia Coyle, provides more information for those interested in delving into this powerful form of meditation.) The talking circle is not only a way to heighten the group coherence but also another way to relate to "the field" or the Tao of nature.

Awareness is engendered by the intention of the group and of the inward bound journey as well as gentle reminders of its principles. To open our hearts we must be aware of and in control of our lower chakras and the sometimes undesirable qualities of judgment, desirous attachment, and ego. Once we modulate these, the heart opens and we connect with the present moment, truth, and self-awareness through love. Now energy can move up above the diaphragm through the fourth, fifth, and sixth chakras respectively, and ultimately to the seventh.

THE IDEAS SUMMED UP IN this chapter and chapter ten are not just theoretical dissertations on universal spiritual principles, but practical ways to enter the sanctuary of wilderness if one wants to connect with the higher self of our inner wilderness. By paying attention to some of these concepts, we can facilitate our journey on the path and that of our companions as well. The heart chakra, compassion, and love are indeed the key to taking the high road in the wild outdoors. Although unconditional love is a major hurdle for all but the enlightened, unconditional positive regard for others is more easily achieved. We need to remember that an aspect of the divine exists in each of us.

The other qualities and techniques of ancient wisdoms we can use to amplify our wilderness journey are summarized and classified as follows:

- Connecting with the cosmos.
- Meditative.
- Dietary.
- Awareness of energy systems.
- Nature and the five senses.
- Group dynamics.
- Shamanic techniques.

CONNECTING WITH THE COSMOS

Be attuned to:

Daily cycles.

Celestial events.

Seasonal changes.

The four elements of earth, water, fire, air.

MEDITATIVE

Mental	Physical
Relaxation.	Yoga.
Reflection.	Tai Chi.
Contemplation.	Dancing.
Meditation.	Walking.
Breath work.	Climbing.
Art.	Swimming.
Writing.	Massage, body work.
Poetry.	Zen-like minimum-impact camping.
Song.	
Prayer.	
Visualization.	

DIETARY

Avoid excess sugar, caffeine, alcohol, and meat.

Eat just enough and eat a nutritious diet.

Consider a fasting solo or vision quest.

GROUP DYNAMICS

No judgment or lavish praise.

Awareness of the shadow.

Transcendence of ego—humility.

Tempered desirous attachment.

Egalitarianism.

Sense of community.

Sharing.

Truth.

Awareness.

Love or unconditional positive regard.

No duality—all for one, one for all.

Wilderness ethics (leave no trace).

NATURE AND THE FIVE SENSES

Smells.

Sounds.

Sights.

Touch.

Taste.

There are more than five senses; to appreciate the sixth and the paranormal we need...

AWARENESS OF ENERGY SYSTEMS

Chakras, nadis, and Kundalini or Num.

Five Sheaths of Patanjali.

Left and right brain, masculine and feminine.

Light and dark.

The Tree of Life.

Other polarities.

Signs and metaphors.

Power animals.

Archetypes.

Primal, primitive, and primeval influences.

SHAMANIC TECHNIQUES

Ceremony.

Rituals.

Chanting.

Drumming.

Sweat lodges.

Pain.

Vision quests.

The power of nature involves the polarity we are able to see at any point during our journey. The balance of opposites is around us continuously: hot/cold; wet/dry; hard/soft; satiated/hungry; exhausted/rested; terrified/tranquil; windswept/serene; dark/light; lost/found; steep/shallow; high/low. In addition, we could add a range of opposing emotions we might feel as we walk the valleys and mountains; the deserts and jungles.

With the meditative effect of wilderness and the help of the group, we are able to integrate these facets like masterful mystics and stay in the middle path as ancient traditions have taught us. The wise trail guide balances these to the group's advantage. No one objects to slogging through the heat if camp is made next to a river and the day ends with a swim. The difficulties of a climb are forgotten if one has an awesome vista from the top. We have a different perspective of a grueling day if it ends in an exquisite meal. We can use the psychological effect of this dynamic to get the most out of our journey. Our basic human nature yearns for contrast to differentiate and feel alive, vital, and vigorous. This is one reason why it is so natural to be in the present moment in the wild outdoors especially in a fresh, new, exotic place. The joy that results from this experience makes it easy to open the heart and contact the higher self.

⌒

FURTHER READING

Chopra, Deepak, M.D. *Perfect Health.* New York: Harmony Books, 1991.

Lad, Dr. Vasant. *Ayurveda, the Science of Self-Healing.* Santa Fe, New Mexico: Lotus Press, 1985.

Rama, Swami, Rudolph Ballentine, M.D., and Swami Ajayah, Ph.D. *Yoga and Psychotherapy, the Evolution of Consciousness.* Honesdale, Pennsylvania: Himalayan Institute of Yoga Science and Philosophy, 1981.

Treadway, Scott, Ph.D. and Linda Treadway, Ph.D. *Ayurveda and Immortality.* Berkeley, California: Celestial Arts, 1986.

Zimmerman, Jack and Virginia Coyle. *The Way of Council.* Las Vegas: Bramble Books, 1996.

CHAPTER TWELVE

CONCLUSION

A S THE NEW MILLENNIUM APPROACHES, it is clear that we need a way to turn inward because everything around us is trying its hardest to turn us outward. We would prefer that the driving mechanism was not a crisis or catastrophe, that we do not have to become mortally wounded in order to go inside. Whether it is a vacation in Hawaii or high-technology medicine, the modern-day condition has pushed us into an almost exclusively outward direction and helped us forget the receptive, intuitive, compassionate, empathetic part of ourselves. The lure of materialism is powerful and will usually prevail unless we take conscious, aggressive steps to counter it.

If we are to look at replenishing ourselves, we must look to different methods or techniques in which to do this more efficiently—methods that help us go inward. Unfortunately, the trappings of modern-day life tend to lead us astray. Even vacations and holidays in nature are likely to result in a more outward, achievement-related activity. Wherever we go to get away from it all, we seem to be confronted with more technology. If we go into the mountains to ski there are people, crowds, chair lifts, and the latest in skiing and clothing equipment. If we find ourselves on the water, there are boats, water skis, jet skiing, wind surfers, and similar trappings to block the inner journey. If we go into the outback it is often with a four-wheel-drive, a camper, cameras, generators, and other paraphernalia to distract us and keep us busy.

It does not matter whether we are ice climbing, mountain climbing, or rock climbing, kayaking or caving, modern-day consumerism dictates a left brain experience. The inner journey is difficult to find, but an awareness of what is required can help. Although many of these outer activities can be done in an internal Zen type of way given the right circumstances and mind-set, this is the exception rather than the rule. We find it difficult to drop our goal-oriented, or ego-affirming, behavior. However, just as we need to connect with our inner healer in order to clear ourselves of medical maladies, our ability to go inward on a regular basis will keep us whole and healthy. The inner journey into the wilderness, or that journey that helps us connect with the hunter-gatherer part of ourselves, can be most restorative. By healing ourselves in this way, we may be more able to link with and help others heal themselves when we return.

Nature can be the panacea for anyone who is prepared to "get out there" because it is spiritually non-denominational, and we can all avail ourselves of its benefits without it offending our cultural conditioning. Furthermore, nature is available to most of us in North America and is inexpensive.

Wilderness rapture occurs when we come into contact with our higher selves while in nature. The higher we climb up the chakra system, the Tree of Life, or the hierarchy of our needs, the closer the contact with the true self and the more profound the experience. The drive toward the higher self is primary and omnipresent even if subconscious in all of us, whether we follow a spiritual path or not. Those of us who love wilderness know that this is a powerful vehicle for inner peace and harmony and therefore seek it out as often as we can. We also all wish for a direct experience with the divine and hence the next question to ask is: Can we be in wilderness in a different way that will facilitate this primal need? Is it enough to just go into the wild and let "the mountains speak for themselves" or can we accelerate our growth process and advance more rapidly on the path of life?

                                                  ⌒

WE ALL HAVE OUR OWN purpose on this planet and the challenge this presents demands we find and follow it with gusto. If we ask the question, "Death asks not, 'what have you?' but 'who are you?' Life's question is not 'what have I?' but 'what am I?' (Swami Rama Tirtha) we will come closer to our truth or vision of ourselves in this world and then realize as we progress along the trail of life that "when you find your place where you are, practice occurs" (Dogen).

The seduction of materialism and consumerism is overwhelming today and these messages promise to be even more insidiously tempting as technology advances, leaving us little time for an inner practice or life transforming experiences. The ego is king and with the help of media sophistication can be even more daunting. We are in the trenches, in the front lines, and wilderness is fast becoming a major casualty. Where will we go to restore, replenish, and heal? The enemy has many allies:

> *The soul* [higher self]... *by reason of lust had become the principle accomplice in her own captivity.*

> Plato

> *Wants, needs and necessities have different characteristics. It is want that is our enemy, and not the need and necessity.*

> *Desires are the source of our miseries. If all desires are assimilated by the one desire of spiritual attainment, then the purpose is solved.*

> Sri Swami Rama

> *Greed is not stilled with money any more than is thirst with salt water.*

> Ksemendra

> *By attributing worth to tangible objects, man becomes attracted to them; attraction to them brings desire for them; desire leads to competition and dispute among men. These reuse violent anger and the result is delusion. Delusion completely overcomes man's sense of right and wrong.*

> Srimad Bhagavatam 11, 14

It is clear that a wilderness retreat, even every three months, will not be enough to maintain equanimity in the work-a-day world. We need to develop some small, meaningful practice of going inward to sustain us.

The ego confronts us in many disguises—one of which is the spiritual materialism and narcissism of the new age. It is like a chameleon and the different shades and colors it takes on can sabotage or hijack our progress. We may think we are progressing on the path when in fact we are not.

> *Friend please tell me what I can do about this world I hold to and keep spinning out!*
>
> *I gave up sewn clothes, and wore a robe, but I noticed one day the cloth was well woven.*
>
> *So I bought some burlap, but I still throw it elegantly over my left shoulder.*
>
> *I pulled back my sexual longings, and now I discover I am angry a lot.*
>
> *I gave up rage, and I notice that I am greedy all day.*
>
> *I worked hard at dissolving the greed, and now I am proud of myself.*
>
> *When the mind wants to break its link with the world it still holds onto one thing.*
>
> *Kabir says: 'Listen my friend, there are very few who find the path!'*
>
> Kabir

> *A mere glimpse of reality can be mistaken for complete realization.*
>
> **Gampopa**

We all ride the roller coaster of life between peaks and valleys, trying to remain as much as possible on the peaks of pleasure and avoid the valleys of despair, not recognizing that they are one and the same. We remain attached to pleasure or pain and have difficulty remaining in the middle path between, where neither extreme pleasure nor severe pain have emotional impact. We remain goal-oriented and outwardly directed. Judgment of others and desirous attachment to material possessions are hallmarks of our predicament.

There are many non-denominational tools that can be used to facilitate the spiritual path and help us turn inward. In addition to meditation and prayer, techniques such as yoga and Tai Chi do not require adherence to any belief system. Just as a horse can be used to get us to our destination, these can as well. The horse is a vehicle of transport, not a religion, and there is no need to believe in or have faith in the horse. One can use it only as an instrument on the journey. This book demonstrates how wilderness and nature also are powerful instruments for going inward. None of these methods are mutually exclusive and in wilderness all of them can be used to augment the process.

It is only when we are committed to at least touching the true self on a regular basis with some form of discipline that we may come to understand that...

> *To know the real Self to be one's own is the greatest attainment, according to the scriptures and reasoning. To know wrongly the non-self, such as the ego, to be the Self is no attainment at all. One, therefore, should renounce this perception of taking the non-self for the Self.*
>
> Sri Sankaracharya

> *God cannot be realized if there is the slightest trace of pride.*
>
> Sri Rama Krishna

> *In the Samadhi (ecstasy) that comes at the end of reasoning and discrimination no such thing as "I" exists, but it is extremely difficult to attain, as "I-consciousness" lingers so persistently. This is why man is born again and again.*
>
> Sri Rama Krishna

It is in wilderness and nature that we can connect with our higher self most easily and come to appreciate the principles of the above statements. The outer wilderness helps us access the inner wilderness of our psyches, but there are many other ways to accomplish this. Nature, however, is extremely powerful, and as our birthright can be made use of in many forms. A regular garden practice might be more useful than an infrequent wilderness excursion.

We can look at the dynamic simplistically in the form of a diagram.

HIGHER SELF

Holds its own center.

Does not depend on material objects.

Does things for their own sake.

Is the space of bliss and harmony.

Transcends ego.

Outer-directed activities (outward bound)		Inner-directed activities (inward bound)

EGO OR SMALL SELF

Depends on material objects or prestige.

Is goal oriented.

Never has enough.

Causes suffering.

Any inner activity will push us more in the direction of the Higher Self. Activities that are outwardly and goal-directed will move us into an ego orientation. If we can subordinate the ego, however, we might get a glimpse of the other reality.

> *Behind my work was ambition, behind my love was personality; behind my purity was fear; behind my guidance, the thirst for power! Now they are vanishing and I drift. I come, mother, I come, in thy warm bosom—floating wheresoever thou takest me—in the voiceless, in the strange, in the wonderland. I come, a spectator no more an actor.*
>
> Swami Vivekananda

Few of us will attain such spiritual heights but we can aspire to do so and emulate the mystical masters of the past both in and outside of the wild remembering that...

> *Wilderness holds the answers to questions we do not yet know how to ask.*
>
> David Brower

The Beginning

INDEX

☽ LOOK FOR THE CRESCENT MOON

Llewellyn publishes hundreds of books on your favorite subjects! To get these exciting books, including the ones on the following pages, check your local bookstore or order them directly from Llewellyn.

ORDER BY PHONE

- Call toll-free within the U.S. and Canada, 1-800-THE MOON
- In Minnesota, call (612) 291-1970
- We accept VISA, MasterCard, and American Express

ORDER BY MAIL

- Send the full price of your order (MN residents add 7% sales tax) in U.S. funds, plus postage & handling to:

    Llewellyn Worldwide
    P.O. Box 64383, Dept. K195-3
    St. Paul, MN 55164–0383, U.S.A.

POSTAGE & HANDLING

(For the U.S., Canada, and Mexico)

- $4 for orders $15 and under
- $5 for orders over $15
- No charge for orders over $100

We ship UPS in the continental United States. We ship standard mail to P.O. boxes. Orders shipped to Alaska, Hawaii, The Virgin Islands, and Puerto Rico are sent first-class mail. Orders shipped to Canada and Mexico are sent surface mail.

International orders: Airmail—add freight equal to price of each book to the total price of order, plus $5.00 for each non-book item (audio tapes, etc.).

Surface mail—Add $1.00 per item.

Allow 4–6 weeks for delivery on all orders.
Postage and handling rates subject to change.

DISCOUNTS

We offer a 20% discount to group leaders or agents. You must order a minimum of 5 copies of the same book to get our special quantity price.

FREE CATALOG

Get a free copy of our color catalog, *New Worlds of Mind and Spirit*. Subscribe for just $10.00 in the United States and Canada ($30.00 overseas, airmail). Many bookstores carry *New Worlds*—ask for it!

Visit our website at www.llewellyn.com for more information.

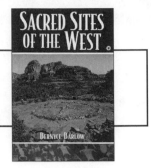

SACRED SITES OF THE WEST
Bernyce Barlow

Stroll through a forest of the world's oldest living trees, explore secret healing caves, or take a midnight dip in the hallowed waters of Big Sur! Sacred Sites of the West takes you on an exciting journey of enchantment and explains how the earth's energies can heal you, rejuvenate your inner energies, and effect your dreams. Investigate ley lines and grid networks, vortexes, and energy wellsprings—all here in the United States! Visit the "Lourdes of America" in New Mexico, tour the inner temple of a Hawaiian heiau, then raft the most treacherous rapids on the North American continent. See the never-before-documented Albino Redwood of California and the Child Nest Rock of Nevada. Dream spots, healing centers, goddess and warrior sites, temples, and vision caves are just a few of the places you'll encounter. Plus, color photographs, holy history, earth physics and legends become an integral part of each site narration, leaving you with a clear understanding of just what makes these sites so captivating.

0-87542-056-6, 240 pp., 6 x 9, 8-pg. color insert, softcover $19.95